Alvar Aalto

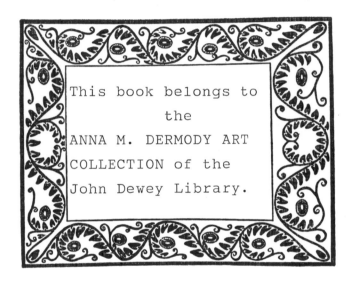

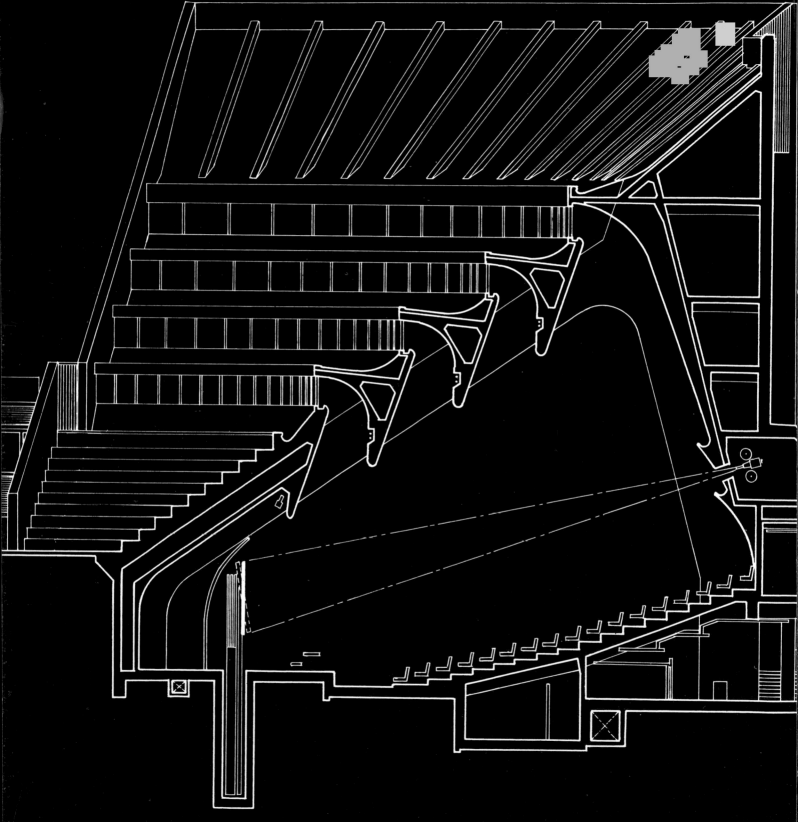

ARCHITECTURAL
Monographs 4

Alvar Aalto

RIZZOLI
NEW YORK

ARCHITECTURAL Monographs 4

Subscriptions and Editorial Offices
7/8 Holland Street, London W8
Tel. 01-937 6996
Publisher
Dr Andreas Papadakis
Editor
David Dunster
Associate editor (France)
Christian Dupeyron
Editorial Board
Alvin Boyarsky, Robert Maxwell,
Robert Stern, James Stirling

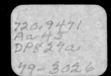

ACKNOWLEDGEMENTS

First and foremost we must thank Mrs Elissa
Aalto and the office of Alvar Aalto (Arkkitehti-
toimisto Alvar Aalto and Co.) for their generous
support. We also wish to thank the Museum of
Finnish Architecture — and in particular their
archivist, Mrs Raija-Liisa Heinonen — for providing much material and the following photographs: p. 33(2); p.36(8, 9); p. 38(3); p. 40(9);
p. 45(10); p. 48(1); p. 60; p. 61(2); p. 68(6, 7);
p. 78(1); p. 79(10); p. 80(3); p. 82(6, 7);
p. 87(1, 2); p. 90(1); p. 91(4). Unless otherwise noted, copyright on all drawings and
photographs supplied by the Museum remains
with the office of Alvar Aalto. Other photographs, except where otherwise noted, are by
Steven Groák, who initiated the idea for the
issue, and without whose constant and diligent
co-operation it would not have been possible.
Drawings used were done by Nadir Tharani,
Peter Beavan, Stefano de Martino, and Ron
Steiner. Thanks must also go to the Finnish
Embassy in London, and their cultural attaché,
Mr Antell. Copyright on Steven Groák's photographs remains with him, as does the copyright
on the essay by Demetri Porphyrios.

First published in the United States of America
in 1979 by
RIZZOLI INTERNATIONAL PUBLICATIONS, INC.
712 Fifth Avenue/New York 10019

Library of Congress Catalog Card
Number: 78-68492
ISBN: 0-8478-0216-7

© 1978 Architectural Monographs and
Academy Editions

Printed and bound in Great Britain

Contents

Front cover
Paimio Sanatorium

Back cover
Finlandiatalo, Helsinki : exterior of main concert hall

Frontispiece
Section through the auditorium, Main Building, Otaniemi Institute of Technology

Foreword

Aalto has remained the most enigmatic of the masters of the Modern Movement. Three solid volumes[1] offering drawings, photographs, and paintings have been published, yet we know that this is by no means the *oeuvre complète.* Somehow he is bathed in the aura of being both a great individualist and one of the two greatest Scandinavian architects of this century, the other being Gunnar Asplund. It is almost as if this aura has pre-empted discussion of the totality of his work, though individual buildings have received thoughtful and penetrating criticism.

It is now time to open up discussion of Aalto's work at the level suggested by Venturi[2], that is, to come to terms with the paradoxes of his work, which since 1927 has been recognisably modern yet not obeying the rules of consistency or expression endemic to the Modern Movement. Work has already begun on the cataloguing of Aalto's remarkable transition from a neo-classical vernacular to his full flowering as a modernist. This path was followed by both Le Corbusier and Mies van der Rohe.

It has already become apparent that the strong silent image of Aalto in his later years was quite different from the boisterous and vocal Aalto of before the Second World War. As more research uncovers more of his own writings, Aalto's image as a Finnish Mies will likewise diminish and disappear as the totality of his work and thought become more accessible. The paradox may become more familiar, even if its does not entirely disappear.

The purpose of including three essays in this issue, thus becomes one of opening up this discussion of Aalto. In the first essay, Demetri Porphyrios discusses Aalto not as the product of a twentieth-century sensibility, but as a mind steeped in the thought processes of the preceding age. Using the concept of *heterotopia,* Porphyrios establishes a tradition not specifically restricted to Scandinavia, of an 'other architecture' of combination and *bricolage* within which Aalto's work may be seen. *Heterotopia* is defined in the Oxford English Dictionary as originating from pathology or biology, and meaning either the conditions for the occurrence of a tumour in some part of the body where it would not normally be expected to occur, or as the conditions of gradual displacement of cells or parts by adaptation to the changed conditions of embryonic existence. Porphyrios introduces this concept, dating in the English language from 1876, in opposition to the term *homotopia,* but both terms fall into the family of nouns dominated by the concept of Utopia. This relation is, however, avoided by discussing not the morality of Aalto's philosophy as expressed in the work but the nature of the ordering sensibility at work. This essay is without doubt a major contribution not only to knowledge of Aalto but also to the theoretical practice of architectural discourse at the present time.

Raija-Liisa Heinonen — without whose wholehearted cooperation neither the work of the contributors, nor the preparation of this issue, would have been possible — extends in her essay our knowledge of the historical backcloth against which Aalto's early work may be seen. Her essay reminds us of the basis of that Scandinavian style which held sway in the fifties and sixties; a basis in the thoughtful consideration of the craft of manufacture. If the results were of less revolutionary nature than the polemics of CIAM or Team X, at least the Scandinavians described an architecture of social democracy by actually building it.

Finally, Steven Groák's essay, a response, though superficially personal, uncovers some conditions and results in Aalto's work of such an order that Aalto's whimsy can be seen to be guided by some logic of the design process. The interconnectedness of the factors which Groák discusses adds up to an interpretation in the best sense providing a coherent narrative of much of Aalto's work.

It was very hard to select which buildings to illustrate. Since the twenties, his office has produced over three hundred buildings and projects. Our selection is grouped under four headings. The first group consists of work from the transitional period. Secondly, there is the exploration of a type, in this case libraries. Then his own office and summerhouse are counterposed with one of his projects for mass housing, and we conclude with a mixed bag of buildings showing the range of Aalto's genius and abilities. This selection is completed by a chronology which is as complete as possible of all the buildings and projects undertaken by Aalto.

While this issue of *Architectural Monograph* was being prepared, the tragic news of the death of Raija-Liisa Heinonen reached us. Without her, the issue would have been impossible. Accordingly this *Architectural Monograph* is dedicated to her memory.

Notes

1 K. Fleig (ed.), *Alvar Aalto I 1922–62,* Zürich, 1963 ; *Alvar Aalto II 1963–70* Zürich, 1971 ; *Alvar Aalto: Synopsis,* Zürich, 1933.

2 R. Venturi, *Complexity and Contradiction in Architecture,* New York, 1966.

Opposite :
Boiler House, Otaniemi
Institute of Technology

Heterotopia: A Study in the Ordering Sensibility of the Work of Alvar Aalto

Demetri Porphyrios

Foucault quotes Borges quoting a certain Chinese encyclopedia in which it is written that '. . . animals are divided into: a) belonging to the Emperor, b) embalmed, c) tame, d) sucking pigs, e) sirens, f) fabulous, g) stray dogs, h) included in the present classification, i) frenzied, j) innumerable, k) drawn with a very fine camel-hair brush, l) et cetera, m) having just broken the water pitcher, n) that from a long way off look like flies.'

In the wonderment of this taxonomy, what makes us laugh is the breaking of all criteria with which we are accustomed to sort out the wild profusion of existing things. We are all familiar with the disconcerting effect of the proximity of extremes or simply with the vicinity of things that are thought to have no relation to each other. The disorder that runs through the Chinese enumeration (or better, the peculiar order that to our eyes looks a mere disorder) consists precisely in the fact that the common ground on which such meetings would have been possible has itself been destroyed. In short, what renders this taxonomy impossible to our minds is the removal of any constant criteria that would enable us to operate upon things, putting them in order, dividing them into classes, or grouping them according to names that designate their similarities and differences.

According to what grid of identities, similitudes or analogies are we, then, to sort out so many different and similar things? What is that space of valuation that allows certain things to cohere and others not? What peculiar rationality allows us to ascertain that these things are similar and those not? The present study is an attempt to analyse exactly that experience: I am concerned to show the ordering sensibility that governs the work of Alvar Aalto and I propose to trace it in the following constitutive areas of architectural production, namely, 1, the planimetric and sectional syntax (the organisation of the plan and the section); 2, the *taxinomia* of function (the classification of the programme); 3, the *taxinomia* of sensuous representation (the organisation of the iconographic themes).

The Planimetric Syntax

It is true that well before the Modernist ethos of the 20s and for a number of centuries — from which we have not yet emerged — the notions of order and geometry have been kept in alliance. Order had been conceived of as the rediscovered portrait of geometry, and vice versa, until the two bathed in the density of their identical shadow. It is within the same problematic that the moralists of Modernism conceived of order as the geometrical austerity of a severe and homogeneous syntax.[1] In his Crown Hall, Mies van der Rohe goes one step further, and by completely denying planimetric syntax to the point of extinction, he reduces the building to the status of its peripheral skin. Pushing the structure towards the borderline of the periphery, a universal aula is born whereby the universality of its imaginary grid guarantees the immaculate homogeneity of its looks, its

Throughout the essays the bold numbers in the margins refer to illustrations, light numbers in the text refer to notes.

1 Crown Hall, Illinois Institute of Technology, Mies van der Rohe, 1956: main floor plan. By denying planimetric syntax to the point of extinction, Mies reduces the building to the status of its peripheral skin.

2 Snyderman House, Fort Wayne, Indiana, Michael Graves, 1970: second floor plan. Graves attempts the fragmentation of the cube through a seemingly confused distortion which is never allowed to slip into inconsistencies, since the decision to fragment aims at disturbing the realm of sameness, but without ever betraying the unity of the whole.

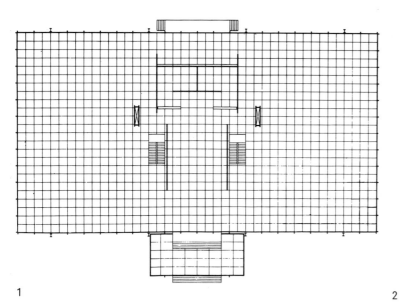

1

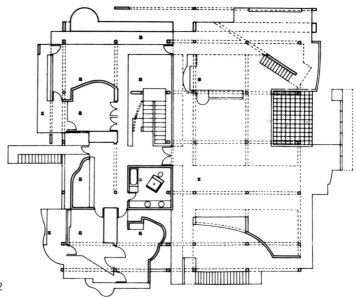

2

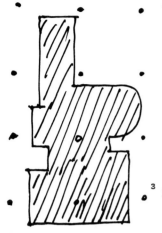

3

3 Maison à Stuttgart : sketch by Le Corbusier from *Oeuvres Complètes, 1910–1929*. Le Corbusier systematically applied the grid/gesture couple as a syntactic device whereby, within the homogeneous space of the grid, the task was to particularise.

4 Cultural Centre, Wolfsburg, Germany, Alvar Aalto, 1958 : ground and first floor plans. Autonomous syntactic fragments are juxtaposed one next to the other without relational reciprocities, but cohering merely through spatial adjacency.

texture, its feel and even its smell. It is as if, by gridding space, one safeguards against all accidents or indiscreet intrusions and instead establishes an idealised expanse in the name of sameness. Were it not for the sudden intervention of a curtain wall, that magic screen of the grid could in fact extend forever, enveloping the whole world and cleansing it of all irregularities.

Before Mies, but with a parallel passion to homogenise, Le Corbusier had systematically applied the grid/gesture couple whereby, within the homogeneous space of the grid, the task is to particularise. In fact, the grid/gesture couple is very similar to the notion of the hero in the classical drama, where the hero's temporality is the sole temporality, where all the characters are subordinate to it, where all incidents are tailored to its measure, where even his opponents are construed as his doubles. In an effort to particularise the universality of the grid, Le Corbusier introduces the singularity of the gesture which, however, can assume relevancy only in as much as it is related to the grid, and which for that reason remains always its prisoner and temptation. The only way by which the Corbusian gesture can individualise itself is by transversing the finite fabric of variations, allusions, dependencies, contradictions, shifts, rotations, transgressions, or resemblances that are already dormant in the grid. This discourse which the twentieth century opens about and around the grid/gesture couple is systematically being revived today through the work of the 'Five' : in the Snyderman Residence, Graves attempts the fragmentation of the cube through a seemingly confused distortion which, however, is never allowed to slip into chaos, since the decision to fragment aims at disturbing the realm of sameness but without ever betraying the unity of the whole.

The necessity for homogeneity, a necessity the character of which is both constructional and ethical, defined the ordering sensibility par excellence of Modernism : *homotopia*. This is the kingdom of sameness ; the region where the landscape is similar ; the site where differences are put aside and expansive unities are established. Homotopias afford consolation ; they favour continuity, familiarity and recurrence, becoming the untroubled regions where the mind can stroll freely, always discovering little hidden clues alluding to the sameness of the universe.

At the other extremity of ordering conceptions there exists a sensibility which distributes the multiplicity of existing things into categories that the orthodox glance of Modernism would be incapable of naming, speaking or thinking. I mean that peculiar sense of order in which fragments of a number of possible coherences glitter separately without a unifying common law. That order, which western rationalism mistrusted and has derogatorily labelled disorder, we will call *heterotopia*; this word should be taken in its most literal sense : that is, the state of things laid, placed, assigned sites so very different from one another that it is impossible to define a common locus beneath them all.

If the homotopic mind set as its task to establish the frontiers of an uninterrupted continuity, heterotopia will now seek to destroy the continuity of syntax and to shatter the predictable modes of the homogeneous grid. In the Wolfsburg Cultural Centre, a number of geometric coherences seem to have been brought together by chance : the radiating grid of the lecture rooms, the introverted arrangement of the library, and the uneven orthogonal grid of the offices, common facilities and auxiliary spaces. Here discontinuities are welcomed. The homotopic requirement of a continuous order is discarded and instead great leaps are introduced. Syntax is not graduated, never shaded. Instead, empty spaces and sudden gaps circumscribe the limits of every region, breaking up the

4

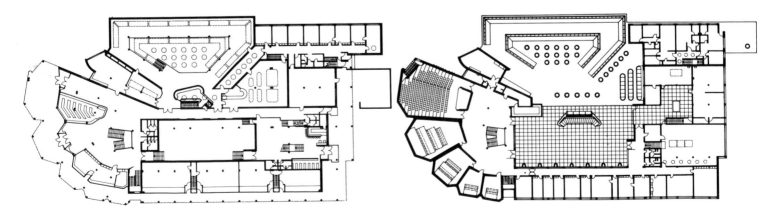

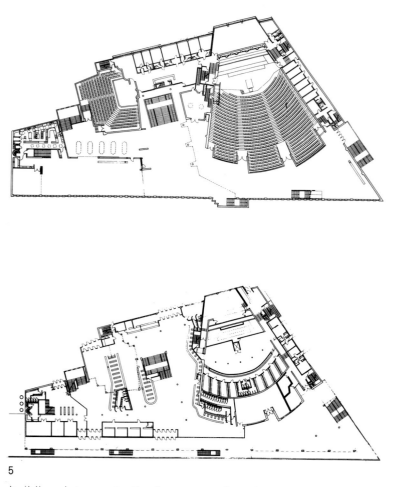

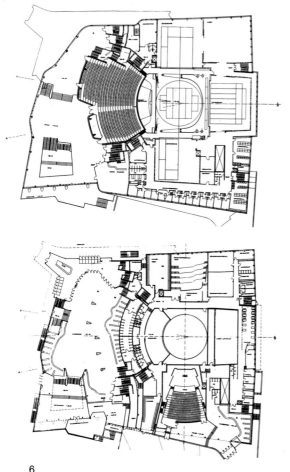

5

6

building into syntactic fragments, then juxta-
posing these fragments; giving no clues that
might account for the lost puzzle; leaving
nothing behind but traces difficult to decipher.

Thus, if homotopia was an ordering sensibility
growing out of its own devotion to link, and by
linking to guarantee continuities, heterotopia
will now grow out of the predilection to always
circumscribe the autonomy of every ordering
gesture, while, by assuming the ever-changing
criteria of an aphasiac, it will always refuse to
relate. Withdrawn into their own suzerainty, the
5 two theatres of the Finlandia Hall, the linear
repetitions of offices and preparatory rooms, and
the empty expanses of foyer space, remain
motionless, yet quivering in outlines, fragments
and pieces. The ordering grids of the two
theatres are personally individualised, while
the foyer spaces are dotted with seemingly
random columns giving the appearance of a
forested region one is to stroll through casually.
These foyer regions are analogous to the
circulation gaps in the Wolfsburg Cultural
4 Centre or the competition entry for the Essen
6 Opera House, and become the empty buffers
that neutralise the tension between dissimilar
geometries or shifted grids. Around this array of
highly personalised localities a skin is stretched
that aspires to delimit the frontiers of the
building, and by so doing, to relate the individual coherencies by default and on the

basis of simple spatial proximity. Thus, if in the
Wolfsburg Cultural Centre things are rubbing
shoulders to an extent that they cohere by their
indiscreet neighbourhood, in the Finlandia Hall
and the Essen Opera House loose fragments are
fenced to be saved from dispersal.

It is enough for the moment to indicate the
principal categories that determine the heterotopic sensibility: *discriminatio* and *convenientia*.*
Discriminatio refers to the activity of the mind
which no longer consists in drawing things
together, but, on the contrary, in discriminating,
that is, imposing the primary and fundamental
investigation of difference. *Convenientia* refers
to the adjacency of dissimilar things, so that they
assume similarities by default through their
spatial juxtaposition. Heterotopia, therefore,
though by nature discriminatory, achieves
cohesion through adjacency: where the edges
touch, where the fringes intermingle, where the
extremities of the one denote the beginnings of
the other, there in the hinge between two things,
an unstable unity appears.

The heterotopic sensibility of Aalto we have
attempted to sketch is neither an individual
expressionism (that is, a secretly lodged
maniera), nor a Dionysian irrationalism, and
even less so a liberating humanistic fugue
labouring the transformation of Modernism.
We would be committing the same historical

5 Finlandiatalo, Helsinki,
Alvar Aalto, 1962: plans of
the main entry and theatre
levels. The heterotopic
ordering sensibility is
revealed both in the
fragmentary planimetric
syntax as well as in the
structural and spatial
vertical discontinuity.

6 Opera House, Essen,
Germany, Alvar Aalto,
1959: plans of main entry
auditorium levels. Around
an array of highly
personalised localities, a
skin is stretched that
aspires to delimit the
frontiers of the building,
and by so doing to relate
the individual fragments
by default and on the basis
of simple spatial proximity.

*The concepts of *heterotopia*,
discriminatio and
convenientia are used by
M. Foucault in *The Order of
Things*, London 1970.

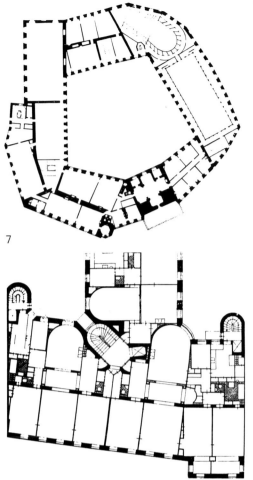

7

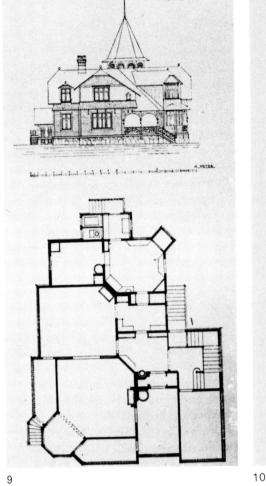

9

10

8

7 Copenhagen Castle after Frederik IV's restoration, circa 1700 : second floor plan

8 Apartment building, Vuorikatu 9, Helsinki, J. S. Siren, 1930. The herbarium par excellence, the collection, where independent spatial and geometric coherences are juxtaposed one beside the other, cohere simply by *convenientia*.

9 Djursholm Villa, Stockholm, circa 1890. The circumstantial planning of the Djursholm villas shares with the American suburb prototypes and the Richardsonian tradition an equivalent heterotopic order.

10 Architect's Villa, Strandagernej 28, Maleren, J. F. Willumsen, 1906

fallacy as Sigfried Giedion — not to mention the array of minor historians who in the 50s contributed to the mystification of Aalto's work — were we to agree that *'... by about 1930 the new means of expression* (iron and ferro-concrete) *had been attained* (allowing Aalto) *to strive for further development and to dare the leap from the rational-functional to the irrational-organic.'*[2] To mythologise Aalto under the straightjacket of 'irrational-organic' is to render him impotent as a thinker and teacher, assigning him the remedial role of a humanistic genius, while contributing neither to an understanding of his work nor to that of its relationship to Modernism. Instead, it reveals the inadequacies of a totalising art-historical mind searching always for a contemporaneous *zeitgeist,* never accepting the contradictions that survivals necessarily introduce in history.

On the contrary, it would be sound to argue that the heterotopic sensibility in the organisation of the plan is a consciously rational ordering gesture, and it seems to have had a persisting appeal amongst the architectural thought of late nineteenth- and early twentieth-century Scandinavia, including Finland. The accretional composition of heterotopia, with its primary categories of *discriminatio* and *convenientia,* was a favourite syntactic ethos of National Romanticism — whether in its Finnish or Richardsonian versions, in the *Volk-Kultur-*

Primitiv of Germany, or the Morris, Voysey, Baillie-Scott British examples.[3] The documents of this tradition are numerous : both Frederik IV's restoration of the Copenhagen Castle of circa 1700 and J. S. Siren's Vuorikatu 9 apartment building at Helsinki[4] reveal the deep heritage of the heterotopic sensibility. These above all are the spaces in which things are juxtaposed : herbariums, collections, species of creatures that present themselves one beside the other, stripped of all geometrical commentary, bearers of nothing but their own individual names. In fact, since the middle of the nineteenth century, the Danish J. D. Herholdt was looking towards the circumstantiality of the additive plan[5] ; and by 1890, in the Stockholm suburb of Djursholm[6], one encounters numerous examples of a consciously mature heterotopic sensibility. The connections with the house of the American suburb prototype are almost unquestionable, especially since it was Johan Henrik Palme who, after an official visit to the United States as Stockholm's town councillor, introduced to Scandinavia the accretional plan both of Olmstead's Riverside houses and those of Richardson.[7] From 1892 onwards, Ferdinand Boberg brought Richardson to the full attention of the Swedes, while a number of articles on Richardsonian buildings appeared in the *Teknisk Tidskrift,* the ancestor of *Arkitektur.*[8] In any event, the architect's Villa of the Danish J. F. Willumsen of 1906 and the ingenious

7
8

9

10

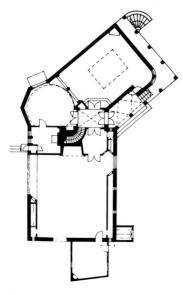

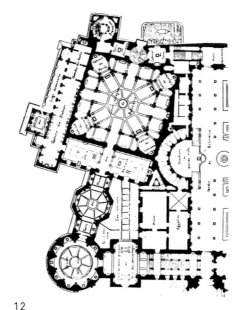

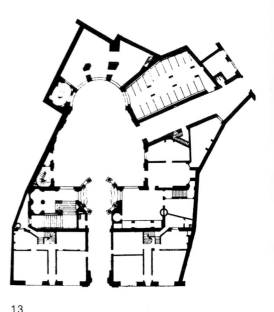

11

12

13

Tarvaspää Atelier of the Finnish Aksel Gallen-Kallela of 1911 are only two of the numerous indices of the heterotopic ordering sensibility that was deep in the vernacular ethos of Scandinavia, Austria, Germany, Holland, and England.[9]

Heterotopia is therefore that ordering sensibility with the curious privilege of discriminating independent coherences, while sustaining a cohesion between the parts only by default and through spatial adjacency. There remains one last clarification. For though heterotopia fragments while simultaneously relating, that act of relating is totally indifferent to any axial continuity. The whole tradition of axial ordering, from the Vatican complex to the virtuosities of the Parisian *hôtel,* even though sharing the same obsession of *discriminatio,* has nothing to do with heterotopia. Whereas the Wolfsburg Cultural Centre relates by spatial adjacency (*convenientia*), the Paris *hôtel* relates by axial reciprocity and the 'highlighted or remembered journey'. Hoterotopia does not compose with allusions, inflections, reciprocities, beginnings and terminations, or implied spatial and diachronic continuities. Heterotopia never commemorates the transition inherent in the joint, never establishes bonds, never duplicates appearances, never remembers the distant glance of composition, never maps out the itinerary of the visitor in hierarchical routes or guiding strides. In its aphasiac silence it commemorates the glittering singularity of the parts, and mends them together in the manner of the Chinese encyclopedist whom Borges has brought to our attention: in the manner of a mute and heteroclite symbiosis.

The Sectional Syntax

Let us search for the syntactic mind that ordered the Finlandia Hall: we discern round, oblong, square, engaged or composite columns, bearing walls that are meticulously aligned and others circumstantially moulded as if by a sculptor.

Every attempt for a relational dependency is here short-circuited, allowing no methodological ambitions to mature. The elementarist ethos of De Stijl or Constructivism — and the subsequent glorification of the syntactic system or method — never touched the mind of Aalto, not even in conjunction with the most controversial issue that was to become the ethical cornerstone of Modernism: the distinction between structural and non-structural members. The column, the bearing wall, and the partition are constantly exchanging identities without any implied system of laws that would account for such a mutation.

In a similar manner, the sectional syntax commemorates the sensibility of heterotopia. Between the ground and first floors of the Finlandia Hall the discontinuity is scandalous: the round columns that sustain the small theatre are suddenly transformed into an undulating wall; the oblong pilasters on the side facing the lake are discreetly internalised into the marble mullions of the curtain wall above; some of the free-standing columns at the acute angle are transformed into engaged pilasters on the first floor, while others disappear altogether leaving no traces in the vertical memory of the building. To the Modernist eye, such sectional discontinuity must have been a gross irritation, surely more iconoclastic than the horizontal discontinuity of the plan. For here the apostolic message of the *domino* — which in a matter of days had become the constructional and architectural best seller of Modernism, winning Le Corbusier the title of *maître* — is at stake. Here the vertical homogeneity of structure is broken into pieces displacing the coordinates of the structural grid, denying the section its spatial continuity, silencing the expectations for the compositional uniformity of the façade, until finally, without any systematic structural, constructional, spatial or compositional dependency, a 'rude' and seemingly primitive stacking takes place.

11 Artist's Atelier, Tarvaspää, outskirts of Helsinki, Aksel Gallen-Kallela, 1911
12 The Belvedere in the Vatican: plan from Julien Guadet's *Elements et Théorie de l'Architecture*
13 Hôtel de Beauvais, Paris: plan from Guadet's *Elements et Théorie de l'Architecture.* The virtuosities of axial ordering from the Vatican complex to the Parisian *hotel* relate the fragmented pieces by the axial reciprocity of the 'remembered journey' and *not* with the spatial adjacency (*convenientia*) of heterotopia.

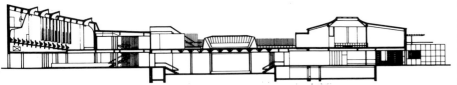

14

14 Cultural Centre, Wolfsburg, Germany, Alvar Aalto, 1958: longitudinal section. The structural, constructional, spatial or compositional dependencies of the *domino* are here shattered, and instead a seemingly 'rude' (to the modernist eye) stacking takes place.

15 Public Pensions Institute, Helsinki, Alvar Aalto, 1952: front elevation and part of the plan at court level. The echelon of the front façade indiscriminately accommodates offices, stairs and corridors, providing no basis for an exterior classification of the programme.

16 Town Hall, Seinäjoki, Alvar Aalto, 1961–2: first floor plan and elevation towards the square. The three superimposed grids of the partitions, structural bays, and window mullions are further disguised by the inconsistent sensuous treatment, thus making the façade the complex condensation of an ever-changing and heterotopic mind.

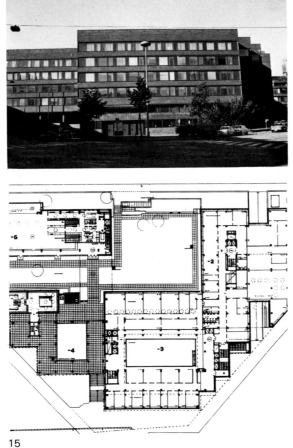

15

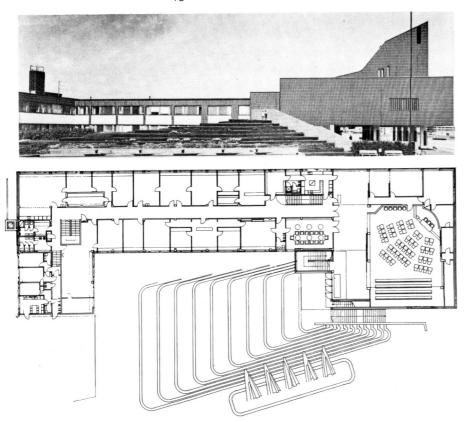

16

The *Taxinomia* of Function

Since the nineteenth century first introduced the category of the building programme and raised the issue of representing utility, architecture never ceased to ask the question: how can a system of designation be established between use and things? Presupposing a thorough classification of functions, such mode of thinking assumed that the distinct coherences the eye is able to articulate as it scans the building's plan, volumetric organisation or sensuous iconography, owe their existence to the respective functions they accommodate. Thus, by means of a superimposed taxonomy of functions and appearances, representation (form) is rendered analysable. In effect, function is to the object one looks at what the cause is to the representation it effects. The Modernist pathos for establishing zones of functions in the plan, for frantically articulating stairs from corridors, columns from non-structural members, or general spaces from specialised ones, has its roots in this alliance between function (utility) and representation; that is, in the obsession of expressing the 'utilisable' with the 'identifiable'.

Aalto seems to be equally unmoved by the classificatory or representational postulates of the functionalist vein of Modernism. What to the Modernist eye was ordered and conceived on the basis of its functional classification, will now occupy foreign regions in the general arrangement of the plan, the volumetric composition or the sensuousness of the façade. In the **15** Helsinki Pensions Institute, the echelon of the front façade indiscrimininately accommodates offices, stairs, and corridors. The programme is thus not perceptible; it provides no basis for an exterior possibility of classification, and therefore it cannot become the common homogenising denominator. The classification of the programme is not to be found in the great expanse of sensuous materiality, while the carcass of the building will no longer serve as the animated screen where its internal life is mapped. Thus, the structural bays do not articulate the façade; the office partitions do not coincide with the structural grid; the mullions are no longer the footprints of the columns behind.

In the Seinäjoki Town Hall, one stair is morpho- **16** logically similar to that of the council room corner, while the other is internalised and accommodated within the office zone. The office divisions do not coincide with the structural bays, the bays do not articulate the façade; instead the latter is ordered by three autonomous yet superimposed grids: those of the partitions, the structural bays, and the window mullions. These three systems are further disguised by the refusal to consistently render them in the same material (wood, copper, or tile) so that they are at least classifiable by their sensuous materiality. Instead, criteria do shift, referentials are superimposed, and the façade becomes the complex condensation of an ever-changing and heterotopic mind.

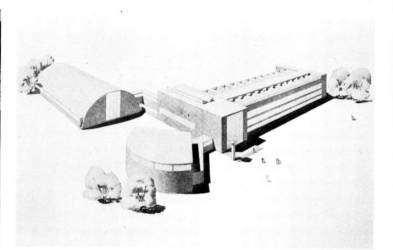

17

18

The functional postulate of expressing the 'utilisable' with the 'identifiable' implied a complete re-evaluation of the Classical conceptions of volumetric composition as well. For Classicism, Renaissance, and the Ecole des Beaux-Arts, volumetric composition was a matter of iconographic literacy and never an issue of systematically applying Functionalism's universal postulate of a monosemantic causality. The gap that separates on one hand Aalto's Paimio Sanatorium and on the other Gropius' Bauhaus in Dessau, the Constructivists' asymmetrically balanced compositions or for that matter, Wilhelm Lauritzen's Zoological Museum project, is of a similar nature. One could be easily mislead by the texts of Giedion and Hitchcock or by the 'preferred' and exhaustively
17 published front façade, in considering the building a Modernist/Constructivist *tour de force*.[10] But there is nothing in the volumetric composition of Paimio Sanatorium that makes it such an exercise. In opposition to Lauritzen's
18 Zoological Museum, which articulates volumes according to a consistent functional taxonomy,
19 Aalto's Paimio Sanatorium blurs the functional clarity of its volumes by refusing to adopt any consistent articulative rules: the stairs are circumstantially either articulated or internalised; the main vertical core or the circulation pattern — with the exception of the patients' wing —

seems intentionally circumstantial and accommodating; while the joints between the various wings are either violent, blurred or articulated without ever any predictable system of laws. Instead, the overall articulative *parti* alludes to the compositional iconography of the *cour d'honneur* in front, and the accretional growth befitting to the ancillary spaces behind. In fact, 20 the only architectural historian who seems to have sensed the reality of Aalto's ordering sensibility has been Reyner Banham who, writing in *The Architectural Review* in 1957, mentions that '*Aalto's . . apparent affiliations to its* (the International Style's) *formal usages and structural methods was coincidental; one might say with literal accuracy, superficial. The back of the Paimio Sanatorium belongs to a different world than the constructivist framing of the side that is so familiar.*'[11]

Though twenty-eight years apart, the Otaniemi Institute of Technology shares with the Paimio 21 Sanatorium the same lust for a heterotopic volumetric composition. It would be in vain to consider reducing the whole area of the visible to a system of variables and then attempt to link them with a functional classification. Instead, the composition presents itself without essential continuity; a visibility that is posited from the very outset in the form of fragmentation, dis-

17 Tuberculosis Sanatorium, Paimio, Alvar Aalto, 1927: front façade
18 Zoological Museum, Nørre Faelled, competition, Vilhelm Lauritzen, 1931: axonmetric. Utility (function) becomes the consistent articulative device for the planimetric and volumetric organisation.

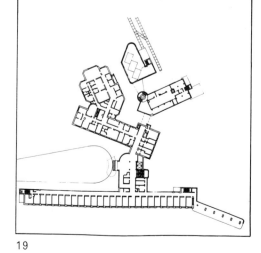

19

20

21

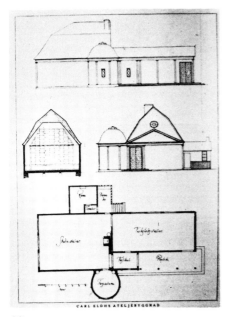

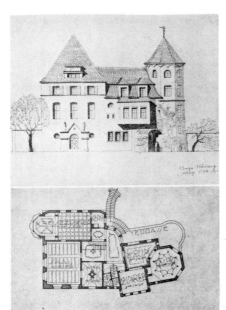

22

23

24

19 Tuberculosis Sanatorium, Paimio : ground floor plan. Utility (function) loses its classificatory suzerainty and instead the compositional iconography of the *cour d'honneur*, and the accretional growth 'befitting' the ancillary spaces behind, become the dominant articulative devices.

20 Tuberculosis Sanatorium, Paimio : view from the service court

21 Main Building of the Institute of Technology, Otaniemi, Alvar Aalto, 1955 main entry from the court. Though twenty-eight years apart, the Otaniemi Institute of Technology shares with the Paimio Sanatorium the same lust for a heterotopic volumetric composition.

22 Carl Edhs Atelier, Ragnar Östberg, 1919. Each room is volumetrically and iconographically articulated, while the building coheres simply by *convenientia.*

23 Hans Römer House, Neu-Ulm, Hugo Häring, 1916

24 Villa Johanna, Helsinki, Selim A. Lindqvist, 1906

25 Hvitträsk Atelier, Kirkkonimmi, Gesellius-Lindgren-Saarinen, 1902

26 House at Stommeerkade 64, Aalsmeer, Bijvoet and Duiker, 1924

27 House at Bergen, J. F. Staal, 1916

28 A. Kittendorffs Villa, xylograf, J. D. Herholdt, 1852

25

26

27

continuity, inconsistency, divergence or discordance.

Yet, long before Aalto, the heterotopic discourse would appear to have been opened in Scandinavia by the idiosyncratic version of National Romanticism, and abroad by the similar sensibilities of Richardson, Frank Furness, Hugo Häring, J. F. Staal, or Bijvoet and Duiker. *Discriminatio* and *convenientia,* supporting one another or ceaselessly conflicting with one another, demarcate the boundaries within which the classicising Edhs Atelier of Ragnar Östberg **22** the medievalising Hans Römer House of Hugo Häring, the National Romantic Villa Johanna of **23** Selim A. Lindqvist, or the Hvitträsk Atelier of **24** Gesellius-Lindgren-Saarinen, are able to define **25** the ordering sensibility of their volumetric composition.[12] This heterotopic sensibility is simultaneously deeper and wider, transcending stylistic classifications, historical contemporaneity or causal attributions : the Dutch Bijvoet and Duiker or J. F. Staal never knew of the Danish J. D. Herholdt, yet their Aalsmeer **26** House of 1924, or the Bergen House of 1916, **27** exhibit the same ordering mind that J. D. Herholdt manifests in his 1852 xylograf of the **28** Kittendorffs Villa.[13]

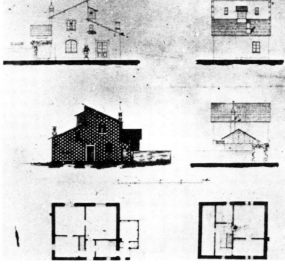

28

29

30

The *Taxinomia* of Sensuous Representation

If Aalto insisted on the fragmentary syntax of the plan and section, on the inconsistent (to the functionalist ethos) accommodation of the programme, or on the agglutinative volumetric composition, he further cultivated a heterotopic tactic in the iconographic treatment of the sensuous aspects of his buildings. In the Jyväskyla Academy, the National Romantic survivals of the pitched copper roof and its simulated dormers inhabit the same land as the Corbusian white *pilotis*, while the immaculate horizontal strips of Poissy co-exist with versions of curtain wall and brick wall. Here, iconographic fragments of a rich historicist consciousness are allowed to spin and twist and mutilate irremediably the homogeneous sameness of Modernism. This indiscreet neighbouring of conflicting iconographic codes is in fact a sensibility that dates back to the tormented but ingenious eighteenth-century mind of Lequeu's 'Rendezvous de Bellevue', and it was systematically cultivated during the nineteenth century under the label of eclecticism. This sensibility is alluded to as late as 1905–6 in the *Architekten* publication on the Villa Oswald by Willy Boch.[14] Here, the wooden cottage structure co-exists with the gothicising tracery, the greenhouse features next to a Romanesque portico crowned by a classicising balustrade,

while in the back the turret of a distant land adds to the exotic flavour of the house. This 'live catalogue' of sensuous representation finds its apogee in Aalto's summerhouse at Muuratsalo where the great variety of brick and tile coursing unfolds uninhibited in the manner of the wild profusion of a quilt. This is par excellence the consciousness of the dossier where things are filed to be saved from extinction; here visibility unfolds in all its spectacle, displaying its similarities, its differences, its associational legends, or its historically burdened sensuous materiality.

This iconoclastic gesture, which Mies could never bring himself to make, does not reveal a new curiosity towards novelty or inventiveness. It is rather, and much more seriously, a mutation in the conceptualisation of the status of the building vis-à-vis the city. For, against the unitary and homogenenous iconography that the internationalist appeal of Modernism promulgated, Aalto chose the 'anachronistic' path of the building as a city. Thus, instead of the singular entrepreneurial image that homotopia cultivated, heterotopia welcomed the symbiosis of a number of conflicting iconographic fragments. In the Wolfsburg Cultural Centre there is no single over-riding iconography. Facing the main square, the horizontal striations

29 Pedagogical University, Jyväskyla, Alvar Aalto, 1950: view of the seminar wings. The National Romantic survivals of the pitched copper roof and the simulated dormers inhabit the same land with the Corbusian white *pilotis*, the immaculate horizontal strips of Poissy or the brick wall and curtain wall versions.

30 'Rendezvous de Bellevue', Jean-Jacques Lequeu, *Architecture Civile*

31 Villa Oswald, Willy Boch, published in the Danish review *Archikten* of 1905–6.

32 Architect's Summerhouse, Muuratsalo, Alvar Aalto, 1953: detail of the courtyard elevation. The great variety of the brick and tile coursing unfolds uninhibited in the manner of the wild profusion of a quilt: this is par excellence the consciousness of the dossier where things are filed to be saved from extinction.

31

32

33

34   36

35

33 Cultural Centre,
Wolfsburg, Alvar Aalto,
1958 : view from the road
34 Cultural Centre,
Wolfsburg, Alvar Aalto,
1958 : view from the park.
The heterotopic sensibility
of ordering is again
manifested : this time
through the fragmentary
profusion of sensuous
iconographies.
35 Students' Association
Building, V. Boulevard 6,
Copenhagen, Ulrik
Plesner, 1909–10
36 House of Culture,
Helsinki, Alvar Aalto,
1955. The office wing is
dressed in the
iconography of a
modernist office block,
the theatre is crowned
with the copper pitch roof
of the traditional civic
monument, while the
porch oscillates between
being a private entry or
a public arcade,
celebrating in this way the
heterotopia of a
multivalent propriety.
37 Jefferson Medical College
Hospital, Philadelphia,
Frank Furness, 1875

37

of green marble, by alluding to the Sienese ecclesiastical architecture, lend the forecourt an appropriate civic splendour. Along the roadside, a caricatured version of the Poissy box elevated on *pilotis* assumes the responsibilities of a street arcade. From the park, an exotic pagoda and the random building fragments that seem to grow from the ground merge their skyline with that of the city, reminding one of its heterotopic image when viewed from the outskirts.

This sensibility, surely indebted to the English block composition, enjoyed great popularity in Scandinavia, especially in the area of tenement housing, as with Ulrick Plesner's Students' Association Building in Copenhagen, of 1909–10.[15] Similarly, the homotopic space of order which displayed representation in a simultaneous table is equally shattered in both Aalto's House of Culture, as well as in Frank Furness' Jefferson Medical College Hospital. It is no longer a question of giving a unitary image, but of restoring at the level of iconography a history of recognisable types. In the House of Culture, the office wing is dressed in the iconography of a Modernist office block, the theatre is crowned with the copper pitched roof of the traditional civic monument, the porch oscillates between a private entry and a public arcade, while similarly, in the Jefferson Medical College Hospital, the wards and clinics retreat to the status of a common residential block, underlining the iconographic prominence of the lecture hall. Thus, instead of being no more than accomplices of a mute visibility of sameness, the theatre, offices, and porch of the House of Culture draft their own plan and section, posit their distinct volumes, and define their individual sensuous iconography not in an attempt to commemorate a Functionalist taxinomia, but instead to celebrate the heterotopia of a multivalent propriety.

The Ideological Instrumentality of Heterotopia

Modern architecture — at least as taught by the aphorisms of the various CIAM conferences or the theoretical texts of its professed historians, and as codified by the socio-economic establishment after the war — was but a coherently worked out manifestation of positivism which, having its roots in the Enlightenment, has ever since remained the faithful and obedient servant of the western mind. Inspired by its eighteenth-century achievements in the field of physical sciences, positivism engulfed the newborn branches of social sciences and linguistics during the nineteenth century, while by the beginning of the twentieth century it succeeded in effecting the bankruptcy of the classical principle of *mimesis* that reigned in the fields of art and architecture. Positivism was thus instrumental in shaping the ideological problematic of Modernism through two equally influential platforms : the scientism of the design process and the socio-economic messianism it promised. Though the second does not concern us here, the first had a number of ideological valorisations vis-à-vis the homotopic ordering sensibility on the basis of which Modernism was able to invest its doctrine with everday recognition and respectability.

With the displacement of the administrative and economic priorities of the west towards controlled and predictable production, the scientistic category of a consistent and systematic methodology was introduced in architectural thinking as architecture's necessary and sufficient design principle, without the latter ever disputing its assigned role as a science. It was in fact the belief that only by transcending its blinded heritage as art could architecture ever be in a position of serving the productive goals of industrialised society. In any case, the moralisation of the decision to align the productive goals of industrialisation with an 'esprit nouveau' had already been debated and won during the nineteenth-century philosphical and art historical vicissitudes of the legacy of the *zeitgeist*. It is, thus, through the displaced categories of consistency and systematic methodology that homotopia emerged — within the 1920s–1950s historical conjunction — as the *modus vivendi* of the International Style, which in practice proved to be a continuously amended version of Miesianism.

On the other side, heterotopia — again within the 1920s–1950s historical conjuncture — played a critical, yet silenced role vis-à-vis western society's priorities. At the level of the planimetric and sectional syntax it negated the constructional codifications that industrialised production necessitated, safeguarding against the absolute standardisation of the building industry and the supercession of the *techne* (technique in labour) by the assembly line. At the level of the taxinomia of function, it stood against the interpretation of architecture as science instead of art, avoiding in this way the quantifiable sterility of Functionalism as well as its secondary and tertiary behavioural consequences that plagued architectural thinking in the 50s and 60s, like the socio-economic data analysis, the user interviews and the rest. At the level of the taxinomia of sensuous representation, heterotopia embattled the entrepreneurial image and the universality of the International Style, not in order to defend regionalism or nationalism, but in order to underline the non-consumability of the architectural object. However, it simultaneously ran the risk of being doubly misappropriated: first, of being misappropriated as an institutionalisation of the collage, the veneer, and by extension the commemoration of the ephemeral world of consumerist waste (as indeed happened with the 'complexity and contradiction affair'), and second, of being misappropriated as an institutionalisation of irrational individual expressionism, and by extension as a mythologisation of the creative genius which industrialised society badly needed in order to reify its corporate goals (as the dominant, even today, interpretation of Aalto shows). That is why Aalto has been denied the possibility of ever becoming a theoretical teacher but instead has always been sketched as the exceptional, yet genial, riddle of Modernism. But he was never a riddle and never a Modernist. At the institutional and ideological levels, the significance of his heterotopic sensibility was, essentially, that it screened off positivism, together with the latter's implicit alliances towards industrialised production and consumerist waste.

Notes

This essay comprises part of the first chapter of my doctoral dissertation, for the preparation of which I was kindly assisted by a grant from the Graham Foundation for the Promotion of the Arts. The study was done under the auspices of Princeton University and I would like to acknowledge my greatest debt and gratitude to the architectural historian Anthony Vidler, my critic and friend, for his especial enthusiasm, devotion and patience in guiding my doctoral studies.

The work has necessitated many visits to Finland and Scandinavia, and I would like to thank all my friends for the hospitality they have extended to me on these occasions. I am especially indebted to Mrs Elissa Aalto and the late Alvar Aalto for the generosity and kindness with which they allowed me to work at the archives of their atelier and for the numerous occasions they were willing to answer my endless requests. I sincerely thank Mrs Maira Gullictchen, Mr Mikko Merckling, Mr Ilpo Halonen, Mr Lahti, and particularly Mrs Raija-Liisa Heinonen, curator of the Suomen Rakennustaiteen Museo, for their assistance, and friendly interest during my research in Finland. I am also thankful to the staffs of the RIBA and Princeton University libraries for the help and privileges they extended to me. Finally, I would like to thank a number of friends — architectural historians and architects — who, having the patience to follow my series of lectures during the 1976 Aalto Moratorium organised by the Architectural Association, helped me clarify in my mind certain issues through their sincere controversy or agreement: Alan Colquhoun, Kenneth Frampton, Dalibor Veseley, Charles Jencks, and Robert Maxwell.

1 In their 1932 edition of *The International Style*, in the chapter entitled 'A Second Principle: Concerning Regularity', Henry-Russell Hitchcock and Philip Johnson write: '*A geometrical web of imaginary lines on plan and in elevation composes the diverse parts and harmonizes the various elements into a single whole.*' In the appendix to the 1966 edition (a reprint of the article written for the August 1951 *Architectural Record*), Hitchcock insists that '. . . *Good modern architecture expresses in its design this characteristic orderliness of structure and this similarity of parts by an aesthetic ordering which emphasizes the underlying regularity. Bad modern architecture contradicts this regularity.*'

2 Sigfried Giedion, 'Alvar Aalto', *The Architectural Review*, February 1950, p.77.

3 The period around 1900 saw in Scandinavia a revival of traditional and peasant styles. Aiming at a rebirth of a national consciousness, the movement has been usually referred to as National Romanticism, and was stronger in Finland, with Gesellius-Lindgren-Saarinen, Aksel Gallen-Kallela, and Lars Sonck as the chief exponents. In Sweden, the prominent figures were Ragnar Östberg, Carl Westman, L. I. Wahlman, Sigfrid Ericsson, and Erik Lallerstedt; while in Denmark, Martin Nyrop, Martin Borch, and later P. J. Jensen Klint. Related to the National Romantic ethos is the deep esteem that Scandinavia had towards the British and German Arts and Crafts, an esteem which, judging from Kay Fisker's article 'Tre Pionerer Fra Aarhundredskiftet' in *Byggmästaren*, 1947, pp.221–232, centred around C. F. A. Voysey, H. M. Baillie Scott, and Heinrich Tessenow, and succeeded in maintaining its strength well into the middle of the century.

4 J. S. Siren's Vuorikatu 9 Apartment Building was extensively illustrated in the Finnish review *Arkkitehti*, Vol. X, 1930. Though stylistically a classicist, as with the Helsinki Parliament or the Helsinki Library Competition (see *Arkkitehti*, Vol XI, 1931, pp. 68–69 and 193–199), J. S. Siren, when faced with the re-conversion of existing structures, addressed in parallel the heterotopic ordering sensibility.

5 For the contribution of J. D. Herholdt towards the fragmentary and additive plan, see K. Varming (ed.), *Dansk Arkitektur, Gennem 20 Aar. (1892–1912)*, Erslev and Hasselbalch, Copenhagen, p. XXVII, '*J. D Herholdt had already commenced to discard the stiff, academic plans. . . . No force was to be used in solving the problem for the sake of traditional regularity.*' Also, see Thomas Paulsson, *Scandinavian Architecture*, Leonard Hill Books Ltd., London, 1958, p. 199, '*Towards the middle of the nineteenth century, it was more common to break up the symmetrical, "classic", facades of Dutch, Palladian, French or Italian origin. The reason was that architects were now abandoning the symmetrical line of rooms in their planning. No special pattern was substituted for the symmetrical; the longing for comfort established the norm.*' And it continues on p.200, '*It is evident that once the principle of a free grouping of the different rooms and consequently of the different volumes of the villa, was accepted, which early happened in the house that Webb designed for William Morris in 1859 and even in Schinkel's House at Potsdam, this freedom was*

then frequently imitated. The emphasis on comfortable furnishings for such houses, much publicised by the Dane J.D. Herholdt in the middle of the century, naturally also contributed to the breaking up of the old symmetrical and formal planning.'

6 For a comprehensive discussion and an extensive illustration of the Djursholm villas, see Gregor Paulsson, *Svensk Stad*, Albert Bonniers Förlag. Stockholm, 1950, Vol. III. In the second volume of the same work, Paulsson shows that the heterotopia of the plan, volumetric composition and iconography also has its origins in the widely practised Scandinavian eclecticism of the nineteenth century.

7 Leonard Eaton, 'Richardson and Sullivan in Scandinavia', *Progressive Architecture*, March 1966, pp.168–171, *'Architectural historians customarily date the international impact of American architecture from the publication of F. L. Wright's work by Wasmuth Verlag, [Berlin, 1910]... However, there is ample evidence to suggest that many European designers closely followed the work of American architects from about 1800 onwards, particularly Richardson and Sullivan. In Scandinavia this is particularly the case... In 1888 Johan Henrik Palme [town councillor in Stockholm] visits USA to look at garden suburbs. He visits Riverside [the outstanding achievement of Frederick Law Olmstead] returns to Stockholm, forms a company and purchases a lot of land at Djursholm [north of Stockholm] for development... The same is true for Saltsjöbaden, another garden suburb, developed by the Wallenberg family in the 1890s... Many of the shingle houses at Djursholm and Saltsjöbaden have a Richardsonian flavour...'* Further, the study, extensively illustrated in plans and photographs, of the American villa that appeared in the *Byggmästaren*, Vol. 16, 1937, pp.368–390, points to the continuing appeal of the heterotopic composition, even after the classical revival of the beginning of this century and the official introduction of Modernism with the 1930 Stockholm exhibition.

8 Leonard Eaton, *op.cit.*, pp.168–171. We know that Ferdinand Boberg went in 1893 to the States, for the Chicago World's Fair. His Richardsonian buildings, the Electric Works at Stockholm of 1892 and the Fire Station at Gävle of 1894, were closely followed by Carl Møller and Ludvig Peterson in their respective Workman's Institute and the Hogonas Store. Also, see Marika Hausen, 'Gesellius-Lindgren-Saarinen at the Turn of the Century', *Arkkitehti*, No. 9, 1967, p.3, *'... when and how Gesellius-Lindgren-Saarinen became aware of the American architecture is not yet known. It is probable, as Kay Fisker has suggested, that the connection went through Sweden, where Ferdinand Boberg's Fire Station in Gävle was well-known, even described in a number of* Architectural Review *found among Lindgren's books.'* The Richardsonian Gustaf Wickman, who was responsible for the Swedish pavilion for the 1893 Chicago Exhibition, continued to cultivate the heterotopic ordering sensibility through a number of illustrated articles in the Swedish review *Arkitektur*, dealing with the accretional composition of vernacular villages in Spain. See Gustaf Wickman, 'Den Internationella Arkitektkongressen i Madrid , *Arkitektur*, 1904, pp.95–105, and also H. J. Molin, 'På Studieresa i Spanien', *Arkitektur*, 1906, pp.42–47.

9 The 1906 Architect's Villa of the Danish Maleren J. F. Willumsen (Knud Millech, ed., Kay Fisker, *Danske Arkitekturstrømninger, 1850–1950*, Ostifternes Kreditforening, Copenhagen, 1951, p.264), or the 1911 Tarvaspää Atelier of the Finnish Aksel Gallen-Kallela share the same typological origin with the 1900 Barn at Exmouth by E. S. Prior (*British Architect*, Vol. 54, 1900), the Tirolian houses of Clemens Holzmeister of the 1920s (*Bau und Werkkunst*, 1924–25, pp.119–120), the Hellerup

Villa by Koch, the 1918 Bendix Villa by the Swedish Louis Hygom (*Arkitektur*, 1918, pp.39–41), or the 1932 Skodsborg House by the Danish Kai Lytthans (*Architekten*, 1932, p.82). The additive aspects of the heterotopic plan of the private house can also be traced in the tradition of the house that is clustered around the fireplace, as in the examples of the 1904 Stocksund House by the Swedish L. I. Wahlman (ed. Sven Ivar Lind, *Verk av L. I. Wahlman*, Svenska Arkitekters Riksförbund, AB Tidskriften Byggmästaren, Stockholm, 1950, p.65), the 1906 Villa at Ryvangs Allé by the Danish Emil Jørgensen (*Architekten*, 1906–1907, Vol. IX, p.421), or the 1924 House at Tirol by the Austrian Welzenbacher (*Bau und Werkkunst*, 1924–25, p.378) and the 1918 Weekend House by Hermann Stiegholzer (*Bau und Werkkunst*, 1928–29, pp.10–11). On the development of agglutinative planning in England and America, see also Henry-Russell Hitchcock, *Architecture: Nineteenth and Twentieth Centuries*, chapter 15, 'The Development of the Detached House in England and America from 1800 to 1900', Penguin Books, 1975, pp.353–381.

10 Henry-Russell Hitchcock, *Architecture: Nineteenth and Twentieth Centuries*, Penguin Books, 1975, p.513, *'[Aalto's] Tuberculosis Sanatorium at Paimio... rivalled the Bauhaus in size, if not perhaps in complexity, and was almost the first major demonstration of the special applicability of the new architecture to hospitals.'* Also, Sigfried Giedion, *Space Time and Architecture*, Harvard University Press, Cambridge, Mass., 1967, p.632, *'As in Le Corbusier's League of Nations Palace, as in the Bauhaus, the various parts [of the Paimio Sanatorium] are fully integrated — like the organs of a body — each having its distinct functions and yet being inseparable from the others*

11 Reyner Banham, 'The One and the Few', *The Architectural Review*, April, 1957, p.244.

12 The Edhs Atelier by Ragnar Östberg was published in the *Arkitektur*, 1919, p.145. For a general text on Hugo Häring, see Heinrich Lauterbach and Jürgen Joedicke, *Hugo Häring, Schriften, Entwürfe, Bauten*, Karl Krämer Verlag, Stuttgart, 1965. The Hvitträsk Atelier by Gesellius-Lindgren-Saarinen at Kirkkonimmi, of 1902, was particularly praised by Carl Bergsten in an article on Finnish architecture that appeared in the *Arkitektur*, 1909, pp.120–121. For a concise discussion of Finnish architecture around 1900, see Kai Laitinen, 'La Finlande au tournant du siècle' and Kyösti Älander, 'L'Architecture et ses Tendances', in the exhibition catalogue *Finlande 1900: Peinture, Architecture, Arts Décoratifs*, Palais des Beaux Arts de Bruxelles, 17 Mai–16 Juin, 1974.

13 For the Aalsmeer House of Bijvoet and Duiker and the Bergen House of J. F. Staal, see Gustav Brandes, *Neue Hollanendische Baukunst*, Carl Schünemann Verlag, Bremen, p.59. The Aalsmeer House of Bijvoet and Duiker was particularly discussed and illustrated in the Finnish review *Arkkitehti*, Vol. XI, 1931, pp.52–54, in an article on Dutch architecture. For the A. Kittendorffs Villa of J. D. Herholdt, see Knud Millech, (ed.) Kay Fisker, *op.cit.*, p.57.

14 The Villa Oswald was published in the Danish review *Architekten*, Vol. VIII, 1905–6, p.49, in an article on 'Rhinsk Arkitektur'. In any event, stylistic eclecticism was cultivated in Scandinavia by the Swedes Axel Nyström and Ferdinand Boberg as well as by the Dane Jens Vilh. Dahlerup, whose 1874 Theatre in Tivoli is a highly accomplished work.

15 See Knud Millech, (ed.) Kay Fisker, *op.cit.*, p.253, *'Christian IV's renaissance of the Netherlands is here rejuvenated by English influence.'* Also, see Tobias Faber, *Danish Architecture*, Det Danske Selskab, (transl. Frederic R. Stevenson), Copenhagen, 1964, pp.145–6.

© Demetri Porphyrios, 1978

Some Aspects of 1920s Classicism and the Emergence of Functionalism in Finland
Raija-Liisa Heinonen

The origins[1] of modern architecture in Finland — and hence of its Functionalist[2] development — can be traced back to the turn of the century. However, the years of World War 1 — and the civil war that followed it — caused a break in architectural development. Until the early 1920s Finland was isolated from other European countries, with the advantage that instead of looking back to the immediate past, architects had to discover a new vision.

The 1920s opened up the borders of Finland. A younger generation had recently graduated, among them Alvar Aalto, P.E. (Pauli) Blomstedt, Erik Bryggman, and Hilding Ekelund. After many years of war and economic depression there were few commissions in Finland and many young architects had to seek work abroad. Ekelund and Aalto went to Sweden, where both found work in offices preparing the Gothenburg Fair of 1923.[3] Ekelund worked at Hakon Ahlberg's office in Stockholm for several months in 1921, and Aalto during the same summer was employed in Gothenburg by one of the main architects of the Fair — Arvid Bjerke. Aalto later claimed that he had designed the large Congress Hall of the Liseberg Tivoli (amusement) area as well as an (unbuilt) smaller theatre. It is more likely, however, that he only took part in their planning because he did not stay for longer than about one and a half months. Bjerke does not record Aalto among his assistants; on the other hand, Ahlberg considered Ekelund one of his most important assistants on his Arts and Crafts Pavilion for the Svenska Slöjdföreningen.[4] Whatever the roles of Aalto and Ekelund in designing the Gothenburg Fair buildings, the time spent in Sweden seems to have been very important for their later careers. They met some of the most talented young Swedish architects, some of whom were also to play an important role in, amongst other things, the Stockholm Exhibition in 1930.

The Scandinavian countries were in close contact geographically, linguistically, and through meetings and periodicals. The predominant language of the educated people of Finland was Swedish, and by the late 1920s some two-thirds of the 154 members of the Association of Finnish Architects (SAFA) still spoke Swedish as their first language.[5] The only architectural periodical in Finland, *Arkkitehti-Arkitekten,* was published in two separate editions, Finnish and Swedish.

Sweden was not the only country to become important in the 1920s. The influence of Italy was even more visible. The curriculum at the University of Technology in Helsinki emphasised Italian Renaissance and Baroque architecture, and it was clear that when young architects were able to travel after the war years, Italy provided their inspiration. In addition to well-known buildings by famous architects, the anonymous vernacular architecture of Italy — the so-called *architettura minora* — proved important.[6] The buildings executed afterwards reflect the Italian sketches of those architects. Nonetheless, many sketches show a more modern expression with their refined cubist forms.

The best examples of this enthusiasm are particularly to be seen in the numerous church competition projects of the period. Many buildings by Bryggman — for instance the apartment house 'Atrium' in Turku (1927) — and the Art Hall in Helsinki (1928) by Eklund and Ekelund, refer to these sources. The Italian *architettura minora* was formally simple and often without ornamentation, though still less cubist than the southern and eastern Mediterranean densely-built, whitewashed, flat-roofed architecture which was introduced by Le Corbusier. Finnish architects' interests in Italian historical architecture was so strong than many new directions of art and architecture, such as Futurism, passed totally unnoticed.

1 Bryggman: Sketch, Fiesole, 1920

2 Bryggman: Apartment house 'Atrium', Turku. Photo G. Welin

3 Eklund and Ekelund: Art Exhibition Hall, Helsinki. Photo Simo Rista

1

2

3

4

5

4 Bryggman: Villa Solin,
Katariinanlaakso

5 H. Tessenow: Housing,
Hohensalza, Posen

6 Carl Christoffer Gjörwell
and Carlo Bassi: Old
Academi Building, Turku.
Photo N. E. Wickberg

7 Ostrobothnian House,
Lapua. Photo P. Kyytinen

8 Aalto: Casa Laurén,
courtyard façade

6

Another important influence was Heinrich Tessenow. Through his architecture and writings some of the ideas of the Deutsche Werkbund were conveyed to Finland. The refined, typified forms preceded also the standardisation which dominated discussion in the mid-1920s. But Tessenow's austere and well-proportioned architecture had something in common with Finnish vernacular. Ekelund,[7] for instance, wanted especially to give prominence to Tessenow's book, *Hausbau und dergleichen* (1916). However, Tessenow's influence could not be seen directly in Ekelund's architecture, but rather in buildings by Bryggman — his Funeral Chapel in Parainen (1929) and his Villa Solin (1927–29); **4,5** and by Gunnar Taucher — communal apartment houses in Helsinki (1925–26). This purified classicism paid no attention to building materials; the architectural effect of the stucco façades — with less and less decoration — was based mainly on good proportions. Classicism cleared the way for Functionalism in this respect, but Finnish architecture was still strongly bound up with traditional approaches.

The architecture of the 1920s in Finland is generally described as 'Classicism of the 1920s' to stress the difference in character between it and the Neo-Classicism of the beginning of the nineteenth century. It recalls more the refined Neo-Classicism of the Italian-born architect, Carlo Bassi, in Turku than the rich Russian-**6** oriented 'Empire' style of Carl Ludwig Engel in Helsinki. The basic forms were often derived from Finnish vernacular wooden architecture, to **7** which classical details were added — garlands, medallions, columns, and arched porticoes. The symmetry and axiality of Classicism was sometimes followed, but more often the plan was designed functionally and freely. This freedom of plan may be traced to Art Nouveau; there was no need to return to the previous restricted symmetry. Aalto's two-family house, Casa Laurén **8** (1925–26), in Jyväskylä, is an example of a building in which the traditional wooden architecture and Classicism are integrated. It is free both in plan and façade. The irregular grouping of the windows on the courtyard recalls Gunnar

7

8

CASA LAUREN

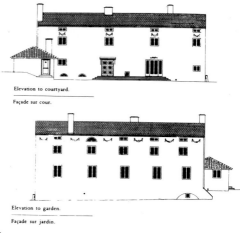

9

10

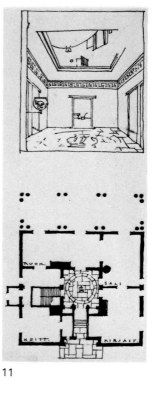

11

12,13

9 Asplund's villa in Djursholmen (1917–18), where an intentional irregularity creates the architectural effect.

Le Corbusier was obviously the first of the pioneers of the modern movement to become known in Finland. His books were reviewed in *Arkkitehti* by Marius af Schultén in 1926,[8] though with no real understanding. Aalto referred to Le Corbusier's ideas in the same year in an article he wrote for the periodical *Aitta*.[9] This article reveals his changing attitude towards Classicism and some of the sources of his later work. It is also an interpretation of the new ideology of architecture presented by Le Corbusier in *Vers une architecture*, published in 1923. But Aalto also combines it with the Italian tradition, as does Le Corbusier. The main picture in the article is Fra Angelico's painting, 'L'Annunziazione', which represented the idea of integrating interior space and nature. The Brunelleschian loggia in this picture is similar to those which Aalto designed the year before in his competition entry for Jämsä church and in the Muurame church, the first drawings being made at about the time that he wrote this article. He also illustrated the article with a drawing of a house for his brother, the Casa Väinö Aalto. The plan is square with a two-storey hall — an atrium — in the centre. The other rooms are grouped around the atrium and those in the

upper floor also open onto it through a gallery. This space is *'the symbol of free open air under the ceiling of home . . . very remotely related to the Pompeian patrician's atrium, the ceiling of which was the sky'*.[9] A Pompeian house accompanies this illustration as does a picture of Le Corbusier's Pavillon de L'Esprit Nouveau. The comparison of Casa Väinö Aalto with a Pompeian house, however, repeats almost sentence by sentence Le Corbusier's chapter, 'The Illusion of Plans',[10] which was also illustrated with the Pompeian House of the Silver Wedding.

Although the idea of joining interior and nature derive from Italian architecture, Aalto clearly had in mind the conditions in Finland, where much time is spent inside because of the severe climate. According to him, *'a Finnish home should have two faces. One of them is the direct aesthetic contact with the exterior, another, the face of winter, is visible in the forms of the interior decoration corresponding to our innermost feelings . . . a uniform, well-connected organism in the garden and the interior . . .'*[11] Later on, this atrium motif — in some cases a piazza — appeared often, though subject to many variations. For example, it can be found in the earlier phases of the Viipuri Library, though in its final, executed version it is hardly recognisable; in the Iron House; in the Academic Bookshop, and in the Rovaniemi, Seinäjoki and other

12

13

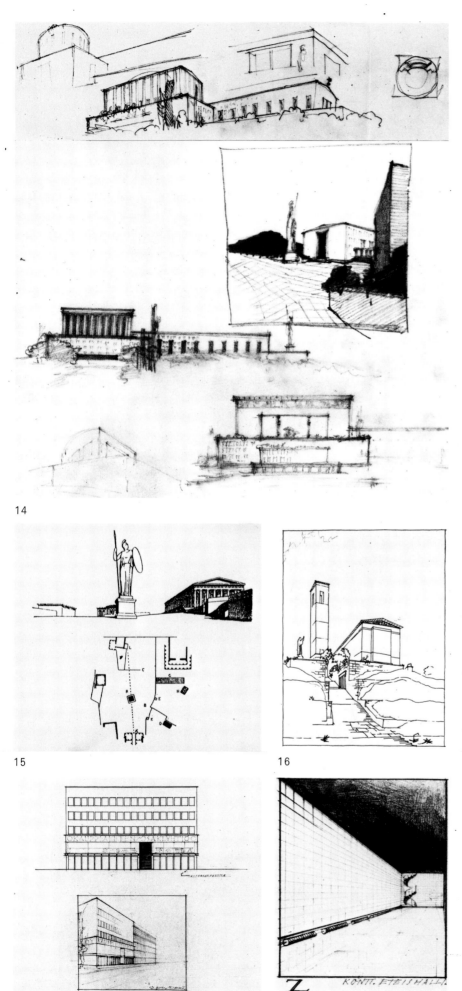

14

15

16

17

18

libraries. In all these he also paid a great deal of attention to natural lighting: all of them exploit skylights to their atria.

Aalto was familiar with Le Corbusier's architecture, but seems to have been more interested in his ideology and the Mediterranean Greek influence than in his formal expression. The League of Nations Palace competition in 1926–27 was to be the turning point: Aalto took part in the competition, but his final project for it has disappeared. Some hundred sketches he made for it reveal a project of extreme classicism.[12] They show two principal motifs: the **14** influence of Asplund's Stockholm City Library (then under construction), shown in the heavy, stereometric mass from which the auditorium rises as a cylinder; and in the idea of the Athenian Acropolis, a large temple surrounded by a ceremonial courtyard with a statue resembling that of Pallas Athene. This Acropolis motif, also illustrated in Le Corbusier's *Vers une architecture*,[13] is to be found in Aalto's succeed- **15** ing competition entries for the Töölö church[14] in **16** March, for the Viinikka church[15] in April, and for the Taulumäki church in Jyväskylä, in July of that year. The results of the League of Nations competition were published in the autumn of 1927, and the disputes it caused made it a matter of discussion among Finnish architects. It is of note that from then on there was a total change in Aalto's architecture.

Another important event was the Weissenhof exhibition in Stuttgart, the same summer. Although it is not known how many Finnish architects visited Stuttgart that year, the Weissenhof Siedlung became well known through publications. The third important event for Aalto at about that time was the move from Jyväskylä to Turku. He had won the competition for the Agricultural Cooperative building in Turku at the beginning of the year. When the contract was signed in June, he had a good reason for leaving the small quiet town of Jyväskylä in central Finland. Turku, by contrast, was a lively cultural and commercial town in those days, and amongst several young architects working there was Aalto's old friend, Erik Bryggman. Moreover, the proximity of Stockholm, with its advanced architectural climate, was a further attraction.

At the end of 1927, Aalto and Bryggman together took part in the competition for the Vaasan Kauppiaiden Oy commercial building with a project that reveals the sudden change in their architectural expression.[16] In many respects **17** it can be compared with Aalto's competition projects for the Agricultural Cooperative building, the Jyväskylä Civil Guard building, and with Bryggman's Hospice Betel. Overall it is more modern and has much in common with the Turun Sanomat, started about a month later: a column visible in the two lower floors; an asymmetrically-placed entrance; a straight staircase leading to the first floor; continuous glazing on the first floor, towards both the street and the courtyard; and continuously-banded windows on the upper floors. Some of the sketches show rich ornamentation around the entrance and on a broad horizontal frieze above the first floor. However, it seems from the perspective drawings that late additions included a spiral staircase, an annexe with continuous window bands, and some very modern interior details. It was as if the architects had learned something new in the course of the competition. Their project was rejected by the jury, because it did not 'follow the rules of the competition'. This reason was not explained. A perspective rendering of their project was, however, published in *Arkkitehti*, together with the prize-winning entries,[17] under the pseudonym 'Waasas'.

Aalto evidently felt it necessary to propagate the new architecture, for immediately afterwards he wrote two long articles. One dealt with social and economical problems of small housing, and was published in a socialist newspaper, *Sosialisti*, at the end of 1927.[18] He criticised the poor quality of housing design and explained the new tendencies in central Europe. The illustrations include Le Corbusier's perspective of the city block of the Ville Contemporaine and J. J. P. Oud's row housing at Weissenhof. The second article was published in a Turku newspaper on the first day of 1928, and included pictures from *Vers une architecture*.[19]

The new ideology of Functionalism became more widely known in Finland in 1928. In April the annual meeting of the SAFA was held in Turku. Sven Markelius from Stockholm was invited to lecture there — most likely at Aalto's and Bryggman's request, especially as they were the hosts of the meeting. Markelius' lecture, 'The Tendencies of Rationalisation in Modern Architecture',[20] advocated the new ideology and provoked great interest among Helsinki architects. Ekelund later claimed that this lecture marked the breakthrough of Functionalism into Finland, for it made the new ideas known to practically all Finnish architects.[21] The following day the *Turun Sanomat* newspaper reported on the contents of Markelius' lecture and also published another article, 'Architect — Reformer', signed by an anonymous 'A'—who may have been Aalto.[22] While its content was similar to Markelius, it was a more unambiguous declaration of the new architecture.

Elsewhere in Scandinavia, these ideas were realised — perhaps a little earlier than in Finland. In Sweden, Uno Åhren explained the new ideology in a long article about the exhibition of the Decorative Arts in Paris, 1925, and Le Corbusier's ideas in another, called 'Towards an Architecture', in 1926.[23] In Denmark, Poul Henningsen started a cultural review, *Kritisk Revy*, which in 1926 began publication with an article by him introducing Le Corbusier's *Vers une architecture*.[24] It seems, however, that

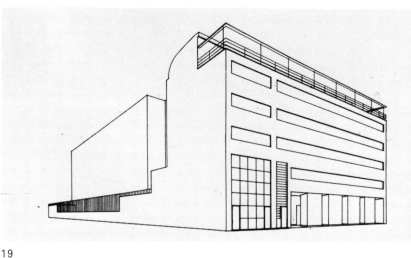

19

Norway was the first Scandinavian country to assimilate the new ideas. Lars Backer had written about them as early as 1925, and his first Functionalist building — the Skansen restaurant in Oslo — was designed in 1925 and completed in 1927.[25] In addition, Johan Ellefsen published in the *Byggekunst* in 1927 a manifesto based on Le Corbusier's ideas.[26]

In the summer of 1928, Aino and Alvar Aalto went to France, Holland and Denmark to see the new architecture. The journey was made by air — 'only 23 hours from Turku to Paris'. Aalto vividly described it afterwards in a Jyväskylä newspaper.[27] Erik Bryggman, together with Ilmari Ahonen from Turku, went to Germany to visit the Weissenhof in Stuttgart, and to Frankfurt-am-Main, where under Ernst May's guidance they saw the housing areas, and to Dessau, where they met Walter Gropius.[28] On his return Bryggman was interviewed by all three Turku newspapers, and explained his views on the new architecture.[29] Thus, the new ideology was introduced to Turku simultaneously from Holland, France, and Germany.

Aalto was commissioned to design a new building for the *Turun Sanomat* newspaper at the beginning of 1928.[30] The building changed little from initial conception to realisation — for example, the columns in the printing hall took on their sculptural form only at the end of the year.[31] The Turun Sanomat is probably the most Corbusian of Aalto's architecture. In fact, it contains 'the five points' of Le Corbusier's 'new architecture'. Aalto was later to develop more personal details and a more individual expression.

The first conflict between the traditionalists and modernists occurred in the competition for the Suomi Insurance Company building, when Bryggman's Functionalist and Yrjö Vaskinen's eclectic projects were placed ahead and considered equal. Bryggman's entry was almost a copy of the Turun Sanomat building, then under construction, or — perhaps more accurately — a further development of the Vaasan Kauppiaiden Oy competition entry. Aalto was a member of the

19 Aalto: The Turun Sanomat newspaper building, Turku

20 Bryggman: The Suomi Insurance Company, competition entry

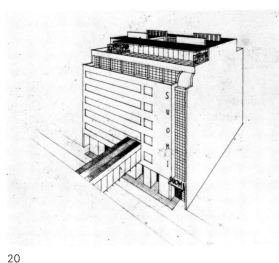

20

jury, and he must have recognised Bryggman's project. He was greatly in favour of it and recorded his minority opinion in the minutes. He also published his opinion in newspapers, expressing once more his ideas on modern architecture. He wrote: *'Many architects think that it is possible, at present, to renew architecture by changing the form and using modern ornamentation. They are eagerly searching for a new style – in vain. Instead of a new style, there will develop an idea, which is not analogous with the word style. There will develop a functional architecture, which implies no special value in ornamentation, but in which the exterior faithfully corresponds with the interior.'*[32] Neither of the projects was realised, though Bryggman was asked to develop his entry somewhat later.

The competition for Paimio Sanatorium, at the beginning of 1929, made Aalto's name among Finnish architects; and when the building was completed, in 1933, Aalto became known internationally. He assimilated at Paimio several ideas from central Europe – not only from the Dutch (Duiker's Zonnestraal sanatorium), but also from André Lurçat (project for a Mediterranean tourist hotel, 1927), [33] Le Corbusier (Paimio's double-height dining room), and Walter Gropius (Bauhaus building). Aalto was also the first Finnish architect to join CIAM in 1929. Markelius also joined at that time and it is very likely that it was he who told Aalto about CIAM. The theme of the Congress, 'Houses for Minimum Incomes', gave Aalto a sound pretext for propagating again the new housing ideas in Finland, whose situation differed greatly from those in Frankfurt-am-Main, Holland, Sweden etc.[34] Building production in Finland was, however, mainly private during the boom at the end of the 1920s, in spite of some promising efforts to start a communal housing programme soon after the war.

For the 700th anniversary of Turku, in summer 1929, Aalto and Bryggman were asked to plan the Commercial Fair area. The architecture was to be a proclamation of Functionalism, with whitewashed, standardised, easily-erectable

stands, and typography similar to that developed in the Bauhaus. Simultaneously, the Stockholm exhibition was in preparation. Asplund was consulted by Aalto and Bryggman and visited the Turku exhibition.[35] The two exhibitions were, however, different – both in their programme and their dimensions. The Stockholm exhibition propagated Functionalism in general but also had a social programme concentrated around housing problems.

The Turku exhibition did not quite receive the attention that Aalto and Bryggman had expected. Only recently has it been appreciated, and is now considered to be the first appearance of Functionalism in Finland. The first exhibition with some kind of social programme was connected with the Arts and Crafts exhibition at the end of 1930.[36] Aino and Alvar Aalto designed a special exhibit for this, called 'The Rationalising of the Small Apartment', in which Bryggman and Blomstedt designed rooms. The exhibition was clearly inspired by the CIAM congresses in Frankfurt and Brussels, and the housing section of the Stockholm exhibition. The catalogue, written by Aalto and Blomstedt, tried to create a positive attitude towards the economic and social questions of housing, and towards prefabricated products. However, it was the Stockholm exhibition that made Functionalism widely known throughout Scandinavia. Practically every Finnish architect visited it, and everybody took a definite stand with regard to it. At least two schools of thought were remarked on by a Swedish critic, Gotthard Johansson, in an article called 'The Romanticism of Helsinki, the Rationalism of Turku', in 1932.[37] In Turku, the architects around Aalto and Bryggman were so-called modernists, while the older generation of Helsinki architects, who had leading posts in the SAFA until about 1932, were traditionalists.

The next conflict arose in 1929, when Armas Lindgren died. He had been the most influential professor of architecture at the Technical University of Helsinki. The easiest solution was to invite Eliel Saarinen to succeed Lindgren. Saarinen had by this time established a considerable career in the USA, to which he had moved in 1923, and therefore did not accept the chair. The vacancy was officially announced at the end of 1929, and by the beginning of the following year only two people had applied for it. One of them was J. S. Sirén, the other Alvar Aalto. Sirén's merits were obvious. He was not only about ten years older than Aalto, who was little known in 1929, but could also present a long list of awards. Above all, his Parliament building in Helsinki was just about to be completed, and it was considered the most important building of the period following independence. Architecturally, it was regarded as a masterpiece – although the younger generation criticised its monumentality and conservatism. In spite of Sirén's evident superiority, selection was postponed till 1931, partly because it had become a

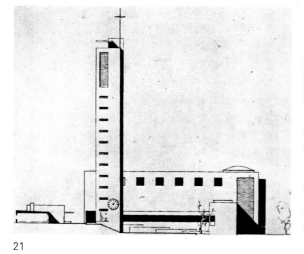

21

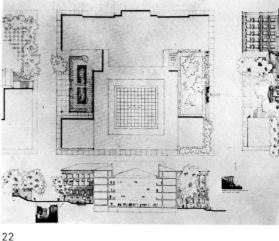

22

21 Bryggman: The Sortavala church competition entry

22 P. E. Blomstedt: The Helsinki University extension, competition entry

23 Aalto: The Helsinki University extension, competition entry

contest between contradictory opinions about the new architecture. Eventually, Sirén was elected to the chair. He was also elected three times to be President of SAFA (1929–31), and he became a regular juror on architectural competitions.

Functionalist projects were highly placed in many competitions during 1928–30. Simply by glancing at the competition drawings published in *Arkkitehti*, one could well conclude that Functionalism had become accepted without any resistance; in fact, the conflict between the older and younger generation continued. The editors of *Arkkitehti* sometimes emphasised their Functionalist leanings by publishing projects they considered progressive. Competition results, however, depended on the membership of the juries. It was often not only a question of selecting the best entries but also of standpoints for or against Functionalism. This became critical,

especially in the many church competitions arranged in those years. Bryggman's entry for the Sortavala church competition won a first prize in 1929, and became something of a model **21** for a modern church. In the Tehtaanpuisto (Mikael Agricola) church competition in Helsinki, 1930, the three first prizes were given to entries which were modifications of Bryggman's Sortavala church — the second prize went to Bryggman — and all were by architects from Turku.

Reaction against the Functionalistic church architecture arose immediately when results were published. It was strongest from the general public, but it soon developed into a direct quarrel among architects. When a new competition was announced for the Tehtaanpuisto church, in which it was required that the church should recognise 'traditional ritual', some traditionalists, such as Lars Sonck and Sirén, were specially in-

Notes

1 This article is based on the author's Fil.Lic. (PhD) dissertation, Department of Art History, Helsinki University, May 1978. (To be published in English as 'The Breakthrough of Functionalism in Finland'.)

2 In Finland, as in Scandinavia, the term 'Functionalism' is generally used instead of 'International Style'. It was mentioned as early as 1928 by Aalto, Bryggman, and P. E. Blomstedt, though terms like 'rationalism', 'neo-rationalism and 'new objectivity' were also used.

3 Interview with Hilding Ekelund, Helsinki, August 1974, conducted by the author and P. D. Pearson; and interview with Alvar Aalto, Helsinki, May 1975, conducted by the author.

4 Sigurd Ericson and Arvid Bjerke, *Göteborgsutställningen*. Stockholm 1930, p. 31.

5 The list of SAFA members. *Arkkitehti* No. 2, 1927, p. 20.

6 Ekelund especially describes the influence of Italy. See his article 'Italia la bella', *Arkkitehti*, No. 2, 1923, pp. 17–28. Also his article 'Rakennustaide ja rakennustoiminta 1918–1947' in *Helsingin kaupungin historia*, Vol v:1, Helsinki 1962, pp. 100–136:

7 Interview with Ekelund, Helsinki, September 1975, conducted by the author.

8 Marius af Schultén, 'Uutta ranskalaista rakennustaiteellista kirjallisuutta', *Arkkitehti*, No. 8,

1926, pp. 152–153.

9 Alvar Aalto, 'Porraskiveltä arkihuoneeseen', *Aitta*, No. 1, 1926, pp. 63–69.

10 Le Corbusier, *Towards a New Architecture* (trans. Frederick Etchells), London 1972, pp. 165–172.

11 Alvar Aalto *op. cit.*, p. 65.

12 The original drawings are held in the Aalto office.

13 Le Corbusier *op. cit.*, p. 174.

14 The entries for the Töölö and Taulumäki church competitions are held in the Aalto office.

15 The original drawings for the Viinikka church are in the archives of the Viinikka Congregation, Tampere.

16 Earlier this competition entry had been regarded as Bryggman's alone, because the final entry was found among his drawings. Recently, a series of sketches was found among Aalto's early drawings, which shows that this entry was designed by Aalto and Bryggman together.

17 *Arkkitehti*, No. 2, 1928, pp. 16–19.

18 Alvar Aalto, 'Pienasunnot — sosialinen ja taloudellinen kompastuskivi', *Sosialisti*, 10 December 1927.

19 Alvar Aalto, 'Uusimmista virtauksista rakennustaiteen alalla', *Uusi Aura*, 1 January 1928.

20 Sven Markelius, 'Rationalisoimispyrkimykset nykyaikaisessa huonerakennustaiteessa', *Arkkitehti*,

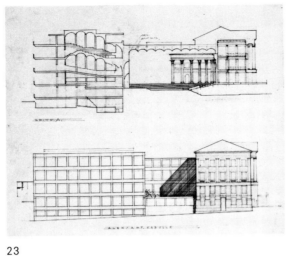

23

vited to compete in this otherwise public competition.[38] Other competitions brought forth contradictory opinions. The most violent debate started between Ekelund and Sirén after the first Tehtaanpuisto competition, both in the pages of *Arkkitehti* and at SAFA meetings. Sirén obviously won this debate by obtaining first prize in the Helsinki University Extension competition in 1931. The annexe he designed was almost identical to the existing Neo-Classical building (1828) by Engel. This was debated in daily papers, above all by Gustaf Strengell, who was against Sirén's project. P. E. Blomstedt's modern **22** entry was bought and it was probably the most interesting of all, with its four-storey-high central hall. Aalto was of course in favour of a modern annexe.[39] And no wonder, for his own **23** project — though partly preserving Engel's large auditorium — presented his new ideas on acoustics and lighting, reminiscent of those in his Tehtaanpuisto entry and anticipating the Viipuri library.[40]

But in the end the reaction against Functionalism, before it had really become established in Finland, was not very strong. It probably followed the lines of the debate in Sweden, conducted after the Stockholm exhibition, but was hardly caused by the kind of political reaction against Functionalism that occurred in Germany and Russia. At the beginning of the 1930s, economic depression hit Finland and very little was built. During this time ideas were to mature. In the following years Functionalism was accepted — though without any ideological or political programme — for nearly all kinds of building. Large residential areas comparable to German Siedlungs were, however, not realised until the very end of the 1930s.

Alvar Aalto's contribution to the introduction of Functionalism into Finland was most important. He was the first Finnish architect to acquaint himself with the new ideology and architecture, to propagate it, and to assimilate it into his own buildings. He also seems to have realised the ideological content of Functionalism without erring in dogmatically following its programme. Even in his most formally pure Functionalist buildings, such as Paimio and the Turun Sanomat, he introduced individual details and in general sought to create an architecture that was in harmony with human life. From the very beginning he believed that: ' . . . *a conscious respect for the problems of our own time in artistic creation implies a mighty goal, to bring industrialisation step by step to the position, which it will no doubt one day achieve — of being a factor for cultural harmony*'.[41]

No. 5, 1928, p. 71, and *Turun Sanomat*, 22 April 1928.

21 Hilding Ekelund, 'Mera om arkitekturutställningen', *Hufvudstadsbladet*, 13 November 1930. Also interview with Ekelund in September 1975, by the author.

22 'Arkkitehti — reformaattori', by 'a', *Turun Sanomat*, 22 April 1928.

23 Uno Ahrén, 'Brytningar', *Svenska Slöjdföreningens arsbok*, 1925. Stockholm 1925, and 'På väg mot en arkitektur', *Byggmästaren*, No. 11, 1926.

24 Poul Henningsen, 'Le Corbusier', *Kritisk Revy*, 1926.

25 Nils-Ole Lund, 'Arne Korsmo og den Norske Funksjonalisme', *Byggekunst*, No. 1, 1966, pp. 2–11.

26 *Ibid.*

27 Jammu, 'Mitä arkkitehti Aallolle kuuluu?', *Sisä-Suomi*, 18 August 1928.

28 Interview with Ilmari Ahonen, Helsinki, February 1974, conducted by the author.

29 *Uusi Aura, Turun Sanomat* and *Abo Underrättelser*, 10 June 1928.

30 Aimo Oristo, *Turun Sanomat, 1904–1954*, Turku 1954.

31 Drawings, dated 31 December 1928, show the sculptural columns for the first time.

32 *Turun Sanomat*, 7 October 1928. The original drawings are in the Museum of Finnish Architecture, Helsinki.

33 This project was published in André Lurçat's *Projets et realisations*, Paris 1929. However, Aalto met Lurçat earlier in Paris and might well have seen this project before publication.

34 Interview with Aalto in the *Turun Sanomat*, 3 September 1929.

35 Eg. *Dagens Nyheter*, 15–16 March 1929 and *Turun Sanomat*, 23 June 1929.

36 'Pienasunto? Pienasuntojen rationalisoimisosasto taideteollisuus-näyttelyssä', Exhibition catalogue, Helsinki, 1930.

37 Gotthard Johansson, 'Helsingforsromantik och Aborationalism', *Svenska Dagbladet*, 9 September 1932.

38 The second competition of the Tehtaanpuisto church was due in November 1932. See eg. *Arkkitehti*, No. 12, 1932, and No. 1, 1933. The competition programme is in the archive of the Museum of Finnish Architecture.

39 *Hufvudstadsbladet*, 14 February and 28 February 1934.

40 The original drawings are in the archive of Helsinki University.

41 Alvar Aalto, 'Uusimmista virtauksista rakennustaiteen alalla', *Uusi Aura*, 1 January 1928.

Workers' Club
1924
Jyväskylä

As originally built, the Workers' Club was free-standing with glazing at entrance level on all four sides (though not continuous). A more recent building now abuts the south side. Within the building an auditorium and foyer are housed behind the stuccoed wall, which sits on the columned and glazed entrance level. Here a restaurant and coffee bar are planned within the structure, which supports the auditorium above; the curved back wall of the auditorium is picked up on a ring of columns completing a circle, with one larger central column reducing the spans to be carried.

Aalto employs various classical devices—Doric columns, the circular 'atrium' space of the coffee bar, the entrance panoply, a 'Palladian' window, and in the original scheme, cartouches to decorate the stuccoed wall. The building implies symmetry on the longer elevation but is in fact only symmetrical on the shorter flanks, a reflection perhaps of the axial symmetry of the plan along the longer axis and the sequence at first floor level of staircase, foyer, and auditorium. The 'Palladian' window is in fact symmetrically placed relative to the auditorium; and while there may not be an overall Beaux-Arts scheme underlying the planning and elevations, there is a square module running throughout the whole building such that all the elements are either squares or multiples thereof.

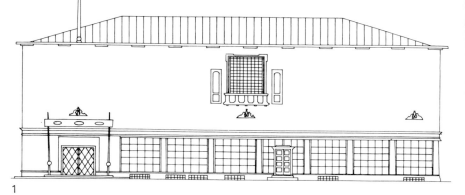

1

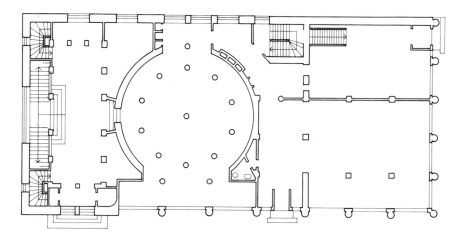

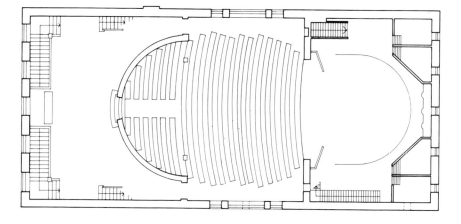

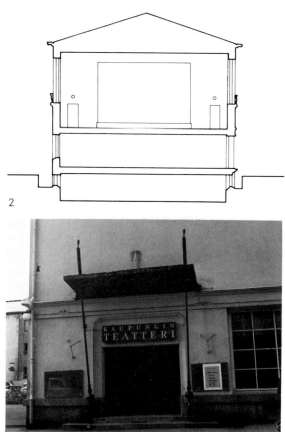

2

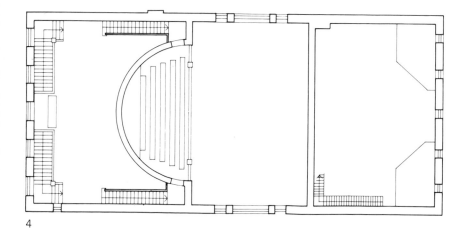

3

4

28

5

6

7

1 Original project : elevation
2 Original project : section towards stage
3 Entrance to theatre
4 Original project : plans for ground, first and second floors
5 Present-day view from the street, showing Palladian window
6 Present-day view from street
7 Canopy support detail
8 Basement window
9 Theatre door handle

8

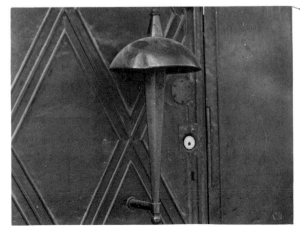

9

Civil Guard Buildings 1925
Seinäjoki

Three buildings were designed for this complex—one containing offices and an assembly room, the others being a stable block and a barracks. The first mentioned building contains a rather grand ceremonial staircase which descends to the assembly, half sunk into the ground, with its flat roof covered with earth, presumably to provide a platform from which the Civil Guards may be inspected. The assembly hall itself is nearly circular, with two enormous Minoan-style pillars off-centre and supporting the wall of the office building above.

The Barracks faces this building across a sandy parade ground and is on the first building's major axis, while the stable block at the other end of the long axis of the site is a symmetrical building but positioned off the site axis. A landscaped semi-circular area completes the site plan at the opposite end to the stable block, producing a neo-classical composition of a kind that Aalto would never return to; the detailing of the elements again shows Aalto's mastery of the language of his elders.

1 Site plan : A Headquarters ;
  B Barracks ; C Stables
2 Headquarters from
  courtyard
3 Headquarters cross section
4 Headquarters plans : lower
  ground floor, upper ground
  floor, first floor

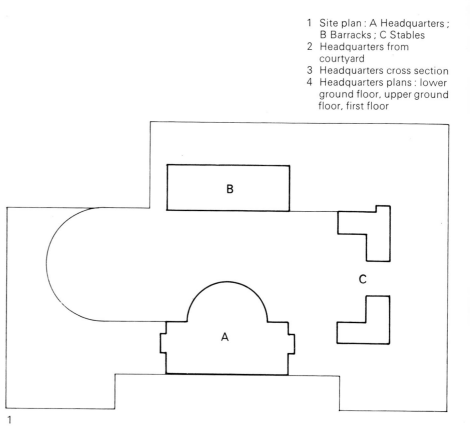

1

2

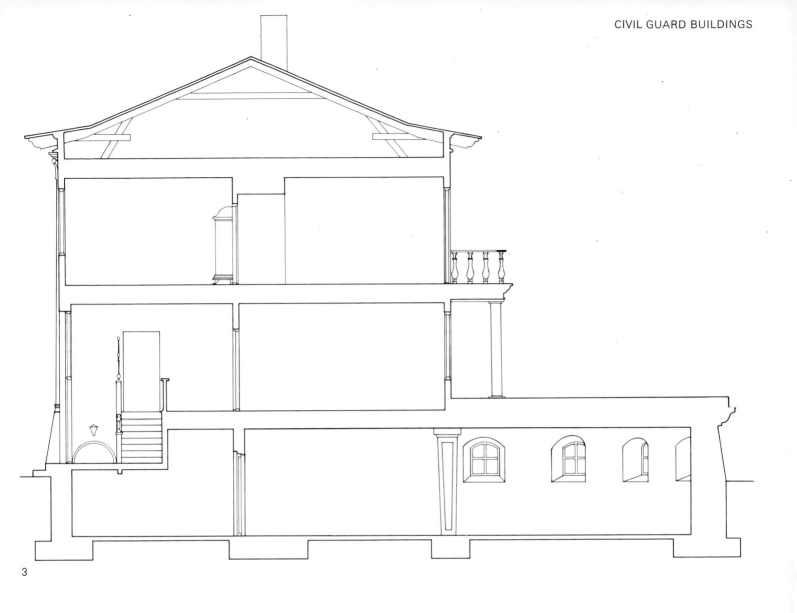

3

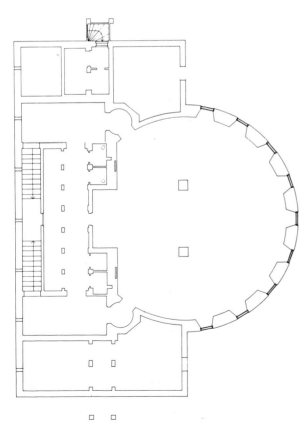
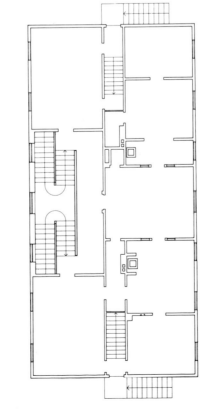
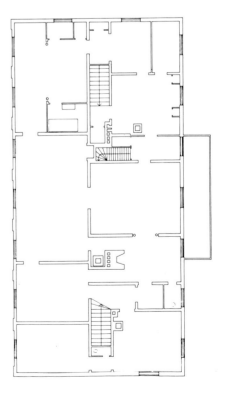

4

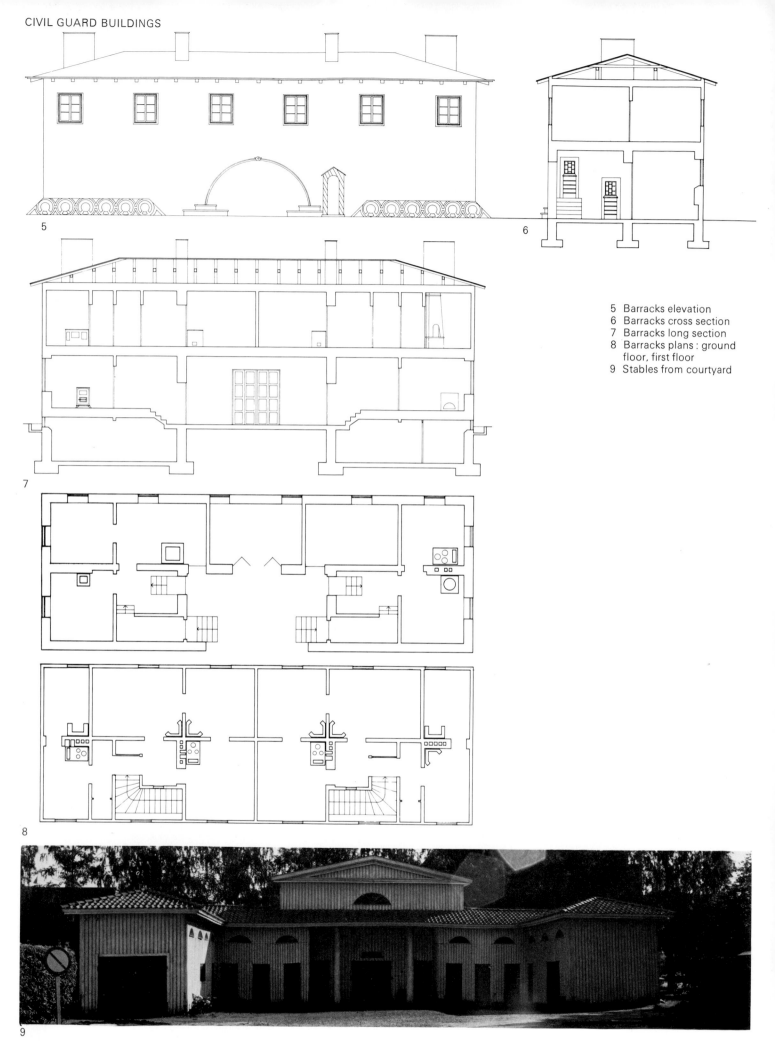

5 Barracks elevation
6 Barracks cross section
7 Barracks long section
8 Barracks plans : ground
  floor, first floor
9 Stables from courtyard

Municipal Library
1927 - 1935
Viipuri, now Vyborg, USSR

The competition project with which Aalto won the competition for this library in 1927 was heavily indebted to Gunnar Asplund's Stockholm Library scheme. The building as constructed avoids the problem of entrance in the first project, where entry is from the angle of an L-shaped courtyard, but extends and refines both the articulation of function and a staircase centrally placed in the library proper.

During the development of the design, the site was changed from being beside a main road to being within a park, a change which allowed Aalto to open up the building to light on all sides. The walls of the building contain a forced-air ventilation system, which confirms Aalto's concern for technical matters, already established at Paimio. This example of the 'wall that breathes'—an idea proposed by Le Corbusier in his Centrosyus block in Moscow, but not carried out in the building—reveals an aspect of Aalto's concerns which has received less attention than his concern for acoustics. The meeting room at Viipuri, with its moulded ceiling, remains one of the most elegant solutions to the problems of acoustics in long rooms with flat floors. It may well turn out, after further analysis, that Aalto's understanding of acoustics was in fact less sophisticated though more obvious than his knowledge and experiments with heating and ventilation.

1

1 Competition scheme
elevation (original site)
2 Aerial view showing
library and nearby church

2

33

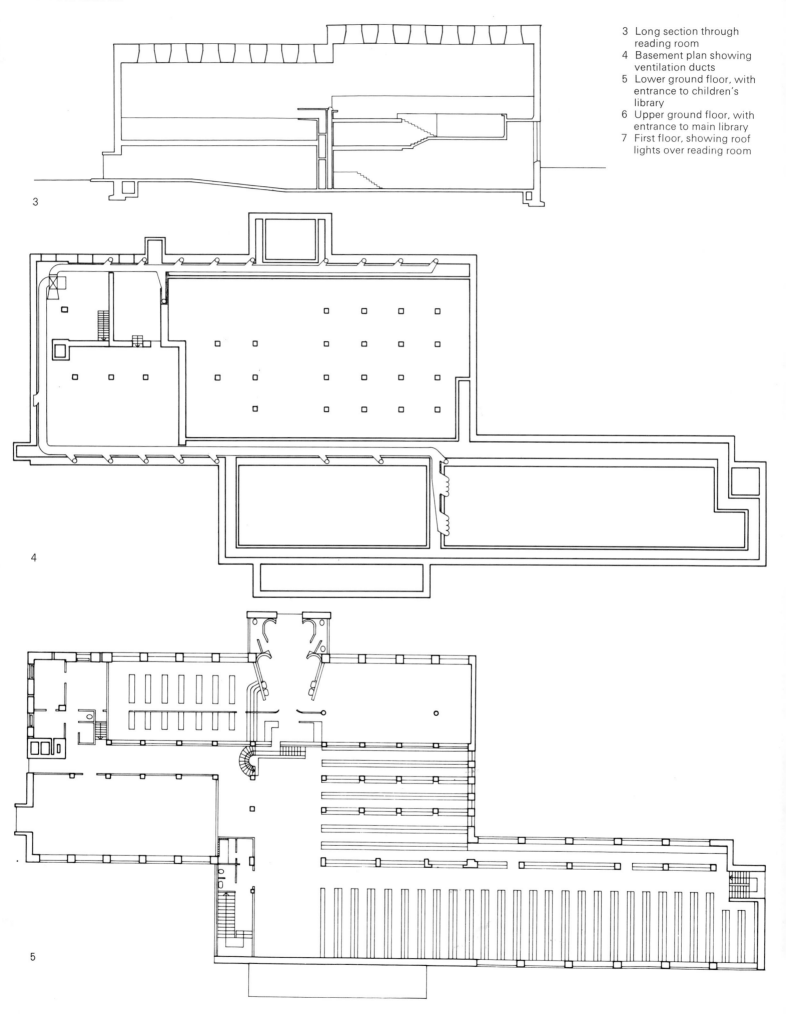

3 Long section through reading room
4 Basement plan showing ventilation ducts
5 Lower ground floor, with entrance to children's library
6 Upper ground floor, with entrance to main library
7 First floor, showing roof lights over reading room

Overleaf :
8 Main entrance
9 Reading room

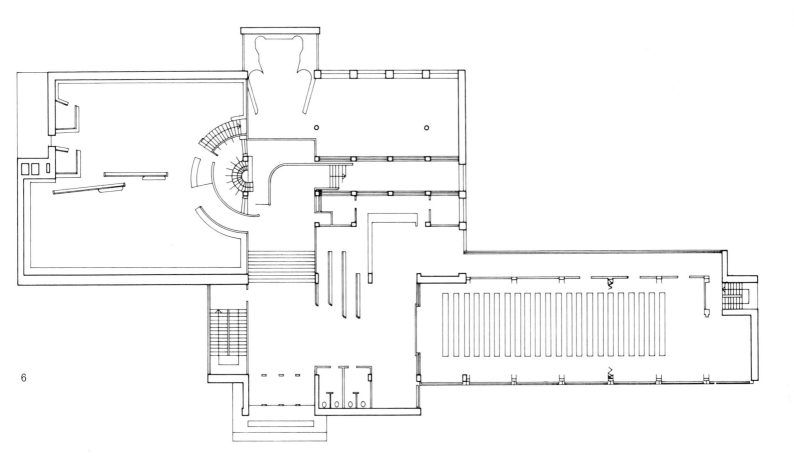

6

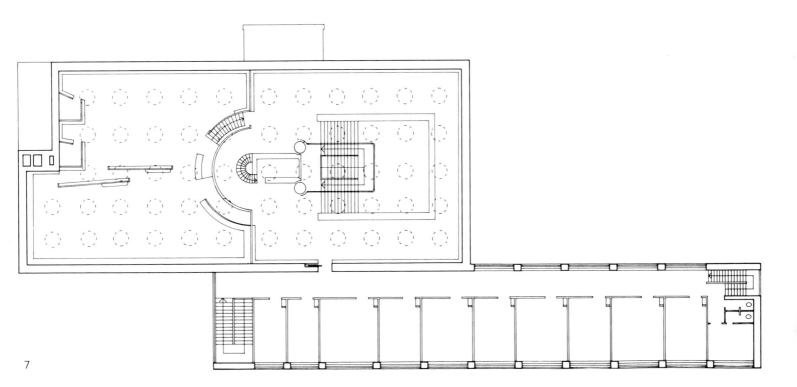

7

8

9

Sanatorium and Housing 1929 - 1933
Paimio

Following the rapid breakthrough Aalto made from a neo-classical style to Modernism, which he had already consolidated in the Turun Sanomat Newspaper Building erected in 1928 in Turku, Aalto entered and won the competition for the Paimio Sanatorium with a positively modern scheme. In terms of its disposition on the site, it follows Duiker's Zonnestral Tuberculosis Sanatorium which Aalto had seen during his visit to Holland in 1928. While Duiker's building is constructed entirely from concrete, however, Aalto uses a reinforced concrete frame only, with the infill being an insulating brick cavity wall which is then rendered and painted white. The sun-trap balconies are cantilevered from the tapering reinforced concrete frame in a way which shows that Aalto was prepared to push the frame to its structural limit.

The whole building complex was justified by Aalto at the time of its completion in a fifty-page pamphlet, in which the design principles are clearly paraded to scotch the fierce attacks from the older generation of Finnish architects.

The scale of the building, its siting, and detailing are all evidence of Aalto's mastery, and catapulted him immediately into the ranks of the Masters of the Modern Movement, and more especially into the ranks of those for whom the expression of function and exploitation of the frame mattered most. A surgical wing was added in the 1950s, and the sun-trap balconies were closed-in more recently, and sadly neither change improves the architectural totality.

1 Aerial view of original scheme (before additions and changes)

1

2

3

2 Back of main staircase
3 Original view from sun
  terrace, showing
  balconies before they
  were closed in
4 Ground floor

4

5

6

5 Junction of communal
block and service block
6 View of sun-trap after
being closed in
7 Typical upper floor

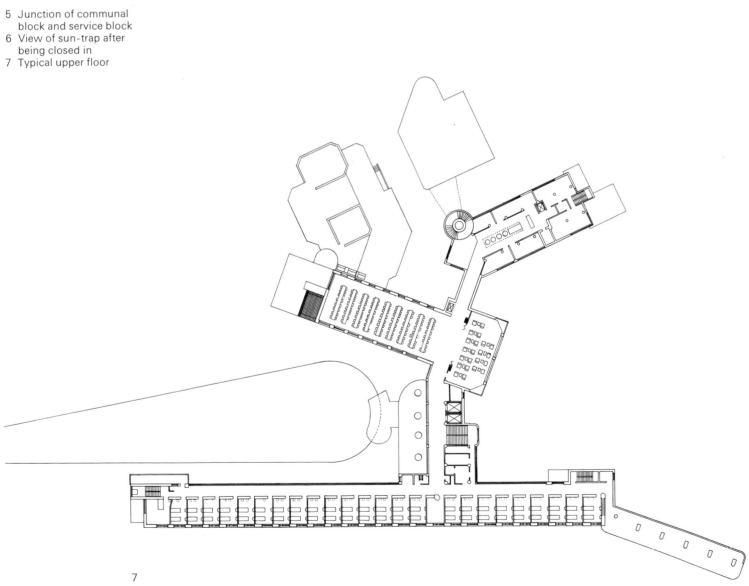

7

8 Surgical block in
foreground, communal
block and ward block
behind
9 Kitchen showing hot air
entrapment system at
ceiling level

8

Opposite:
Entrance hall
Staff dining room, with
coffee lounge over

Overleaf:
Ward block
Present-day view of sun
terrace
Service block

9

10

10 General view of doctors'
   housing, showing
   balconies in their original
   state ; these were
   subsequently filled in.
   (See illustration in List of
   Buildings and Projects)
11 Ground floor
12 First floor

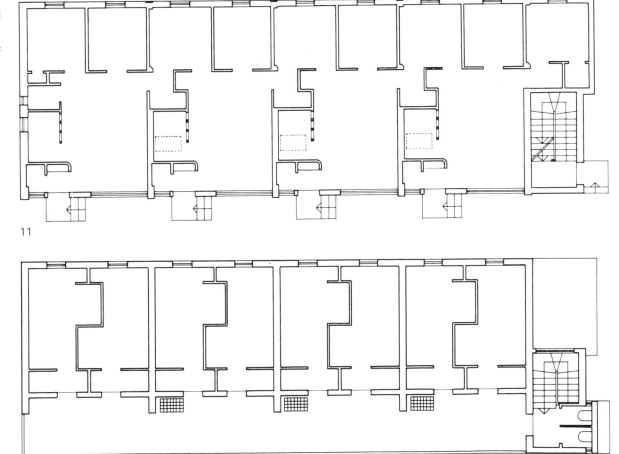

11

Opposite :
Main staircase

12

13

14

13 General view of staff
housing
14 General view of staff
housing
15 Ground floor and first
floor

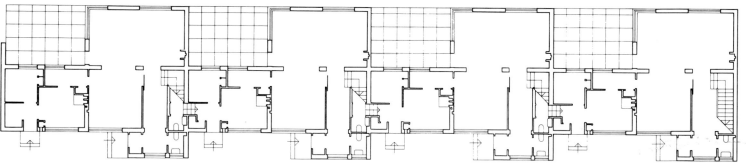

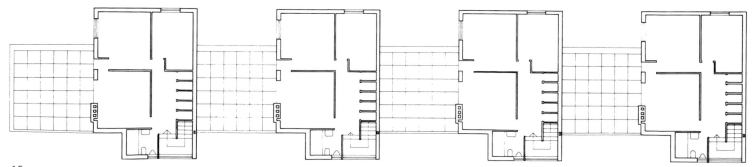

15

University Library Extension Competition 1937
Helsinki

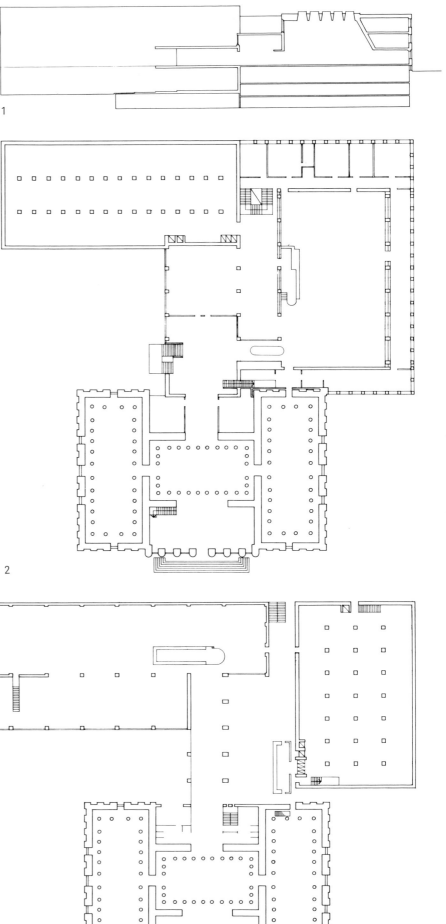

The competition for the extension to Carl Ludwig Engel's University Library (1836–45) was won by Aalto's former pupil and assistant, Aarne Ervi. Aalto submitted two alternative schemes, one of which won the second prize. Like the library at Viipuri, both schemes propose a zoning of the programme according to function, but in one of the schemes a three-storey high reading room is proposed in which a timber(?) soffit flows from the ceiling of the three-storey space down across a wall and into a single-storey space. A system of circular rooflights lights the main space, as does a large south-facing window. It is not clear from the drawings how Aalto proposed to solve either the acoustic problems of such a space or the problems of solar gain and over-heating which would have occurred in that volume.

Aalto's elevations attempted to blend in with Engel's library by continuing ashlar stonework across the base and walls of the project. It may have been this apparent rejection of the plain surfaces of modernism which lost him the first prize, though the idea of using stone to either blend in with surrounding buildings or to make a public gesture of some force was to re-occur time and again in his later work.

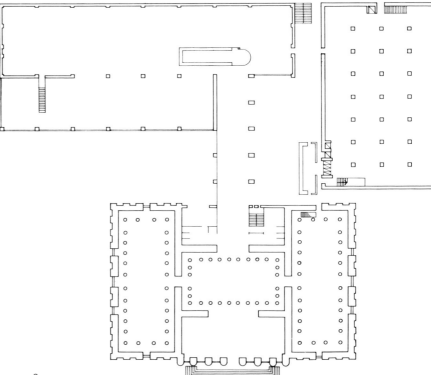

1 Competition, first scheme : section through reading room
2 Competition, first scheme : plan
3 Competition, second scheme : plan

Library, Institute of Technology 1964 - 1969
Otaniemi

The library closes off at an oblique angle the third side of the park/court established by the main buildings of the Institute of Technology, begun twenty-two years previously. As a major reference library, the main problem was to provide good working conditions for the students over a three-storey basement for the library stacks. These spaces, and the small lending collection are housed in a faceted volume on the side, away from the main buildings. In the rectilinear tail of the building, offices and seminar rooms are provided.

Two public entrances coincide at the junction between the library uses and the office and seminar part of the building. One of the entrances faces the roadway, the other the main campus. Because of the complexity of use, the staircases are disposed in a manner reminiscent of Aalto's disposition of stairs in his concert hall and theatre schemes. While continuing the use of the red-brick generally employed in the Institute's buildings, Aalto uses copper for the roof and applique panels of white marble to denote entrances. The columns at the roadside entrance imply classical references in their fluting and base, but not in their proportions. Internally the library spaces do not seem to have the coherence and presence of his other smaller libraries, the repetitiveness of the ceiling plan seeming almost a defeat in the face of the problem of providing individualised spaces for working within what is basically a big hangar.

1

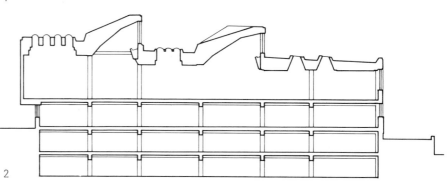

2

3

1 View of reading room,
  showing clerestory lighting
2 Cross section
3 View of the main entrance
4 Plans : lower ground,
  upper ground, first floor

4

Library
1963 - 1965
Seinäjoki

The town centre plan devised by Aalto and now
complete, comprises a block of municipal offices,
a theatre, a library, town hall and parish hall and
church with a belfry interrelated by a sequence
of public spaces. The blank wall of the library
facing south lies opposite the grassed steps
leading up to the courtyard of the town hall. The
façade looking away from the town centre is
horizontally exaggerated by the louvres of the
windows to the main library spaces, and thus
implies a link between the theatre and the church.

A double-loaded corridor block is split about a
third of the way along to provide the focus of the
library, the entrance and control desk. To the left
is the children's library, to the right the administrative offices of the library, and right ahead, a
well in which the reference library is housed; and
around that and beyond, the main stacks of the
library fan out. The roof identifies and contains
the functional separation of elements of the
library, rising in an abrupt curve over the main
stacks to allow light to enter and bounce around
in the space. Externally the roof-line reveals little
of the complexities experienced internally. The
whole building is white, except for its dark skirt-
ing where it touches the ground and the entrance
steps hidden behind a marble slab.

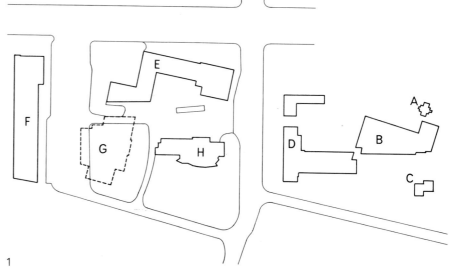

1

2

3

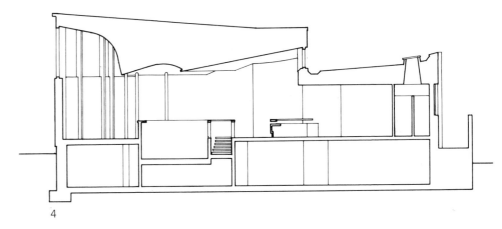

1 Site plan of town centre :
A Bell tower ; B Church ;
C Priest's house ; D Parish
centre ; E Town hall ;
F Local government
offices ; G Site for
theatre ; H Library
2 Aerial view from bell
tower
3 Louvred window to
reading room
4 Cross section
5 Upper ground floor

4

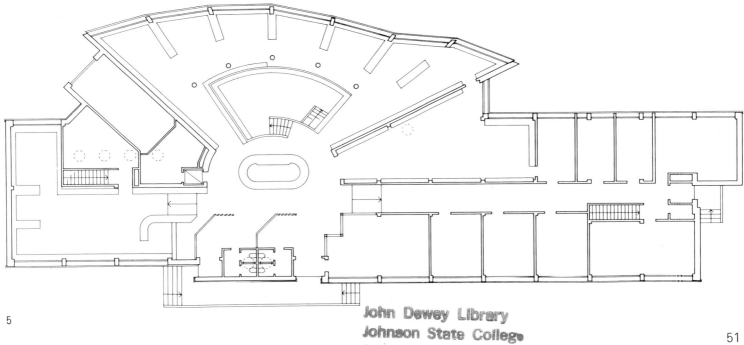

5

6 Window detail (local
government offices
beyond)
7 Reading room, looking
toward main entrance

Opposite:
General view of library, with
town hall and bell tower
beyond
Reading room

6

7

Library
1963 - 1968
Rovaniemi

Apart from functioning as the central library of Finnish Lapland, the building houses workrooms, conference rooms, offices, a cafeteria, a travelling library depot, a small kindergarten, caretaker's flat, lecture and exhibition spaces, and the Arctic Bird Collection.

In the plan of the library, again shaped like a fan, Aalto hollows out a reading/work space at a lower level within each segment of the fan. The library does not therefore suffer from the discipline of the bookstacks, but can instead look like a book-lined space. The resulting effect of horizontality, given by the continuous shelves, provided a basis against which Aalto can play with and distribute both natural and artificial light. Internally the effect of the raised lid of the roof is only given where two roofs are adjacent. Externally the glazing and roofs to the library spaces are absolutely dominant. The libraries are clad in white tiles, laid to give a vertically striped effect, and the rest of the building is rendered.

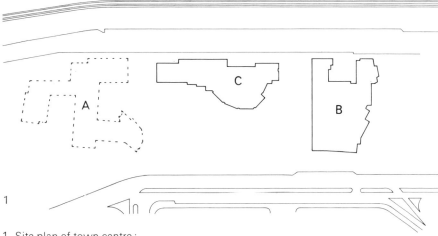

1

1 Site plan of town centre:
  A Site for town hall;
  B Library; C Lappia
  House (theatre);
2 Main reading room,
  looking towards issue
  desk

2

3 Cross section through
  reading rooms
4 Cross section through
  gallery
5 Lower ground floor
6 Upper ground floor

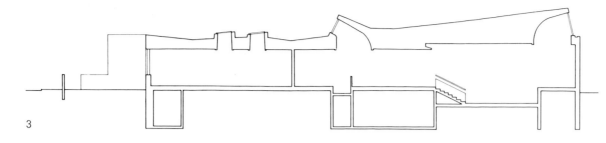

3

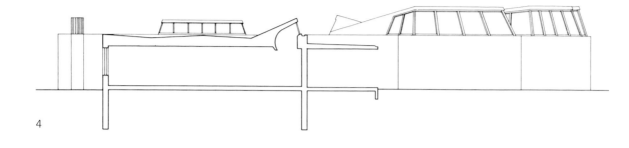

4

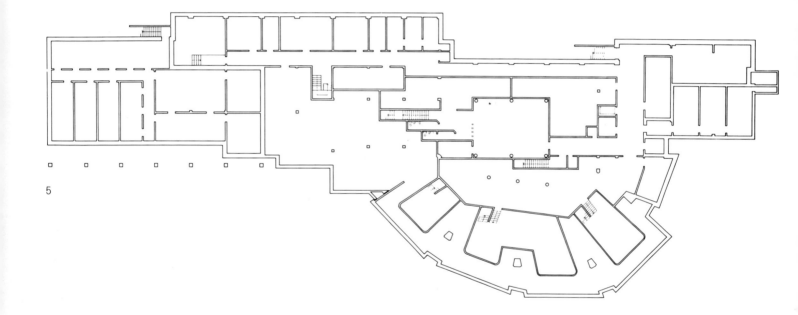

5

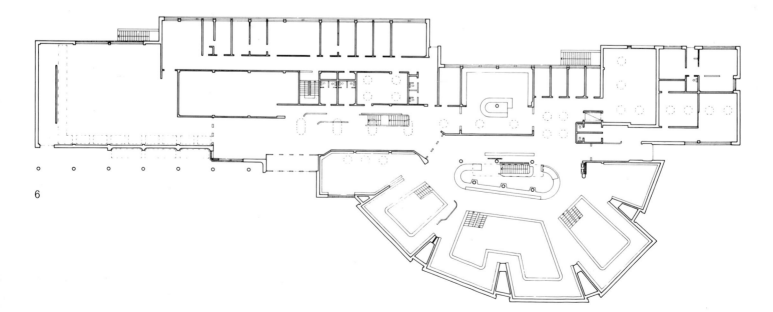

6

7 Gallery
8 Entrance hall, looking
  towards gallery door
9 Entrance hall, looking
  towards reading room

7

8

9

10

10 A small reading room
11 Detail of clerestory to
main reading room

Opposite:
Staircase from main reading
room to lower ground
floor

11

1 Cross section through
  reading room
2 Reading room, showing
  clerestory lighting

Library, Mount Angel Benedictine College 1965 - 1970
Mount Angel, Oregon, USA

The library building is sited overlooking a slope and between two existing buildings. Towards the campus it is single-storey, with the section dropping away to provide the library spaces. The book stacks radiate on two levels from the entrance and control point. A two-storey high rooflit volume separates the stacks from the entrance and contains all staircases.

Workspaces occur at both levels of the library: open desks on the perimeter of the upper level without view but with high-level light, and below, carrels naturally lit with windows running from desk to ceiling and partially blinkered by vertical timber louvres outside. The materials are rough yellow brickwork, the basement cut into the hillside is dark painted concrete, and all window frames are dark hardwood. The roof is copper.

1

2

3 Entrance level (upper
  ground)
4 Lower ground floor
5 Basement

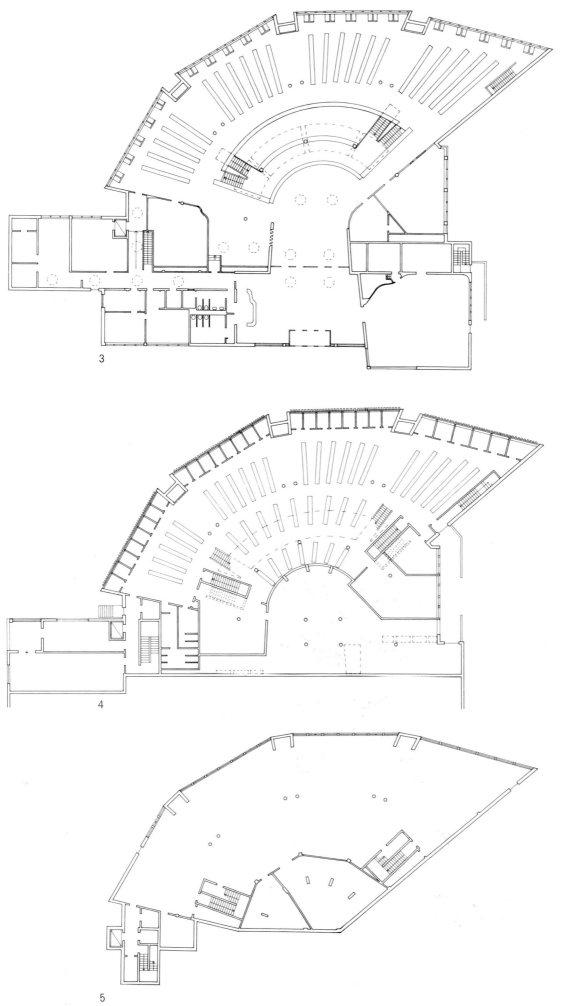

3

4

5

Academic Bookshop
Competition 1962
Constructed 1969
Helsinki

Externally the building is a relatively straight-forward copper-clad curtain wall. The brighter character of the Pohjois-Esplanadi is recognised by lining the window frames with strips of white marble. The two entrances off either street converge under an array of light fittings, from which leads the three-storey space of the bookshop tucked in behind other buildings. Three crystal-line rooflights bring light into this volume, and indeed appear to have embedded themselves in the roof. The vertically striped balustrades of white marble seem to attenuate the height of the space and dominate the colourful display of books.

Three storeys of carpark are housed beneath the bookshop, and offices occupy the building above.

1 Main entrance
2 General view

1

2

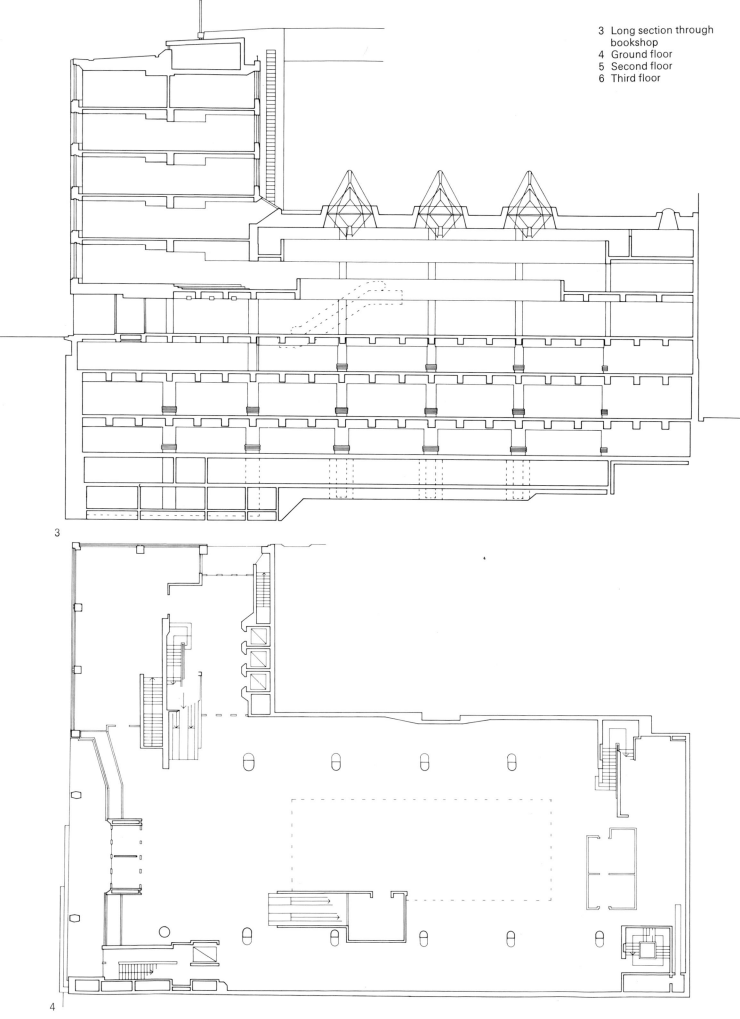

3 Long section through
  bookshop
4 Ground floor
5 Second floor
6 Third floor

3

4

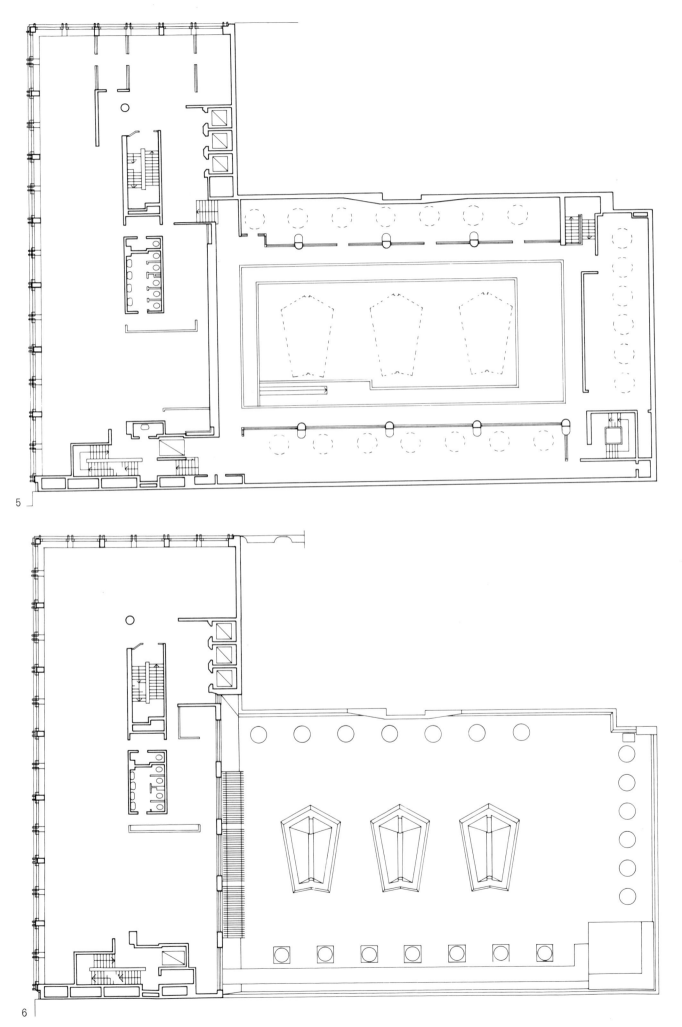

Block of Flats
1965 - 1968
Lucerne, Switzerland

Aalto's efforts at high-rise living are located outside Finland. The first was at the Hansaviertel,
West Berlin (1955–7), the second at Bremen,
also in West Germany (1958–62). At Lucerne,
the fanning motif is once again used, though
with more expression of the service core than at
Bremen. Thirteen floors provide a total of six flats
per floor, with each flat having a different number
of rooms. The penultimate floor contains only
four apartments, two of which are much larger,
and the top floor consists of one luxurious pent-
house surrounded by a nearly continuous terrace.
The building is constructed out of large-scale
prefabricated wall elements in concrete.

1

1 General view. Photo Bob
  Smith
2 Ground floor
3 General view. Photo Bob
  Smith
4 Typical upper floor

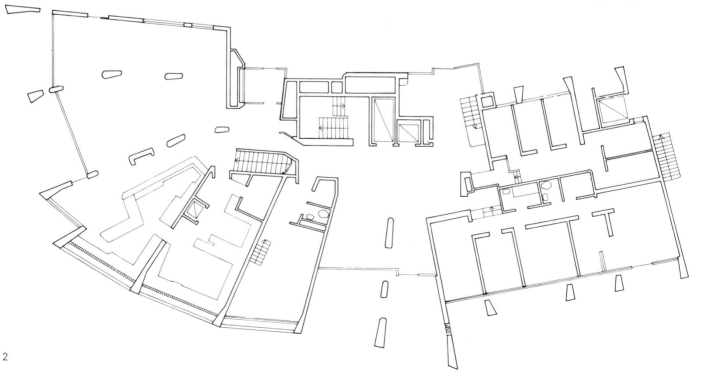

2

66

3

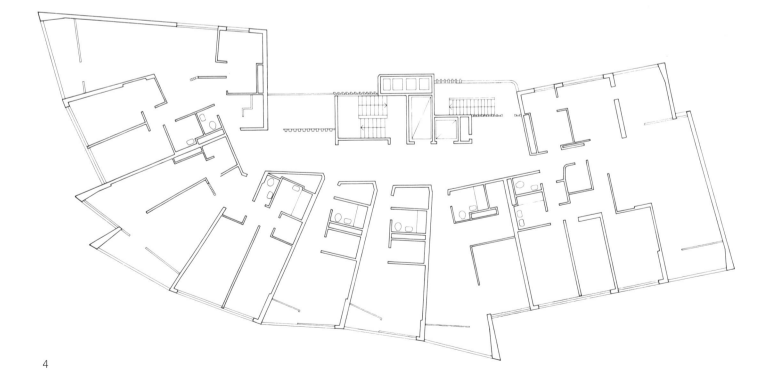

4

Architect's Studio
1953 - 1956
Munkkiniemi, Helsinki

Situated on a corner site in one of the suburbs of Helsinki, Aalto's office resembles more a villa than the conventional image of an architect's working space. This impression is deepened by the 'garden side', where Aalto formalises the contours to create a space which formally and spatially resembles an amphitheatre. The curved wall of the drawing office could be read as the resultant of a pressure from the 'positive' external space, with the concomitant implication that an unseen public are dominating the work of the architects looking out onto this space from their drawing boards. That space is then both an implied public realm and paradoxically the garden of the villa. In restricting himself to this rhetorical gesture, Aalto dramatises what is otherwise a simple and domestic-scale building. The office continues to practise from these quarters.

1

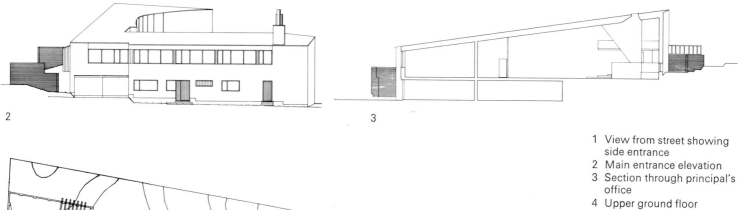

2   3

1 View from street showing side entrance
2 Main entrance elevation
3 Section through principal's office
4 Upper ground floor
5 Lower ground floor

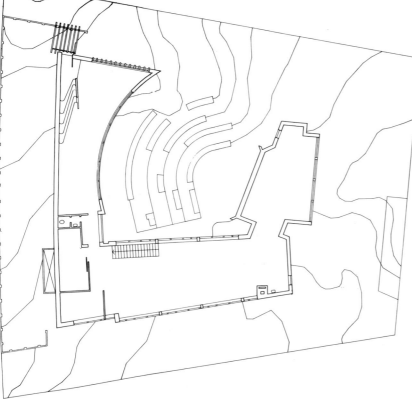

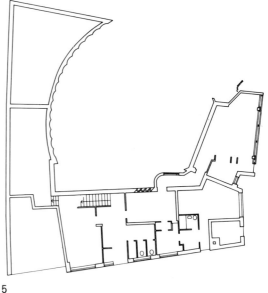

4

5

6 General view of courtyard
7 Principal's office showing side entrance

6

7

Architect's House 1953
Muuratsalo

Aalto's private retreat is sited on the edge of a forest, by the rocky side of a lake. The basic courtyard theme is again used, here tapering off with outbuildings into the forest. The outer walls of the house are brickwork painted white, whereas the courtyard, by contrast, is a *mélange* of varying sizes of brick laid in varying bonds, with some tiling patches as well.

This courtyard has always been explained as an experiment by Aalto in the mixing of materials, and if this is true, it would have been interesting to know which juxtapositions were regarded by Aalto as failures. Since this was never discussed in the documentation printed while he was still alive, it is tempting to speculate that the courtyard is the result of his own desire to express individuality in what, after all, is the most appropriate location. It must be noted that the experiment was never repeated.

1

1 General view of courtyard
2 Site plan
3 Ground floor

Opposite:
Detail of courtyard, showing experimental brick and tile panels
General approach, showing out buildings

Overleaf:
Academic Bookshop, Helsinki

Students' Hostel Otaniemi: general view; and view of main entrance

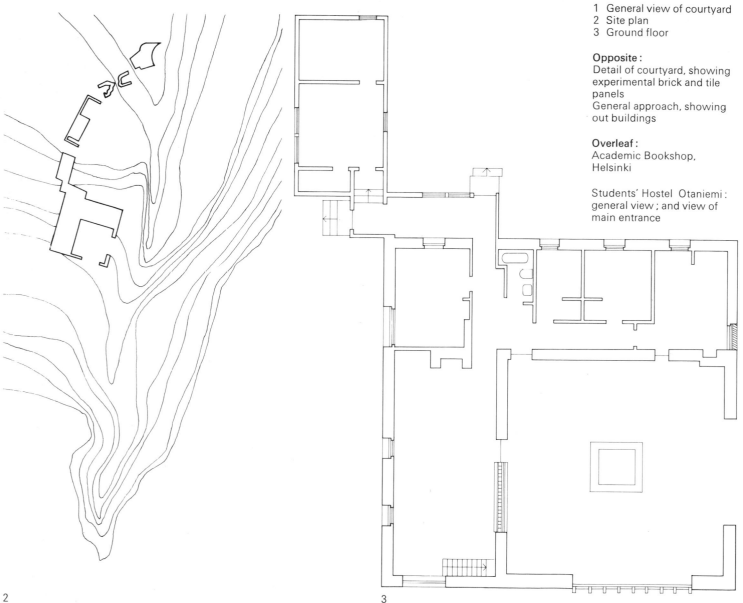

2

3

Lappia House
1975
Rovaniemi

The accommodation of the Lappia House comprises the Lapland Provincial Museum, a music school, a small broadcasting organisation, a multi-purpose theatre seating over 400, and a 150-seat conference hall which can be combined with the theatre to form one volume.

The second of Aalto's buildings for Rovaniemi, the Lappia House, will be joined by a town hall, thus completing the infrastructure of the town centre. While extensive use is made of tiling both externally and internally, the building seems to recall in its massing the Werkbund Theatre, 1914, of Van der Velde.

Opposite :
General view
Detail of main entrance

1 Ground floor
2 First floor
3 Upper level
   (For basement plan, see List of Buildings and Projects)
4 Main staircase leading from entrance/cloakroom area
   (ground floor) to foyer (first floor)

4

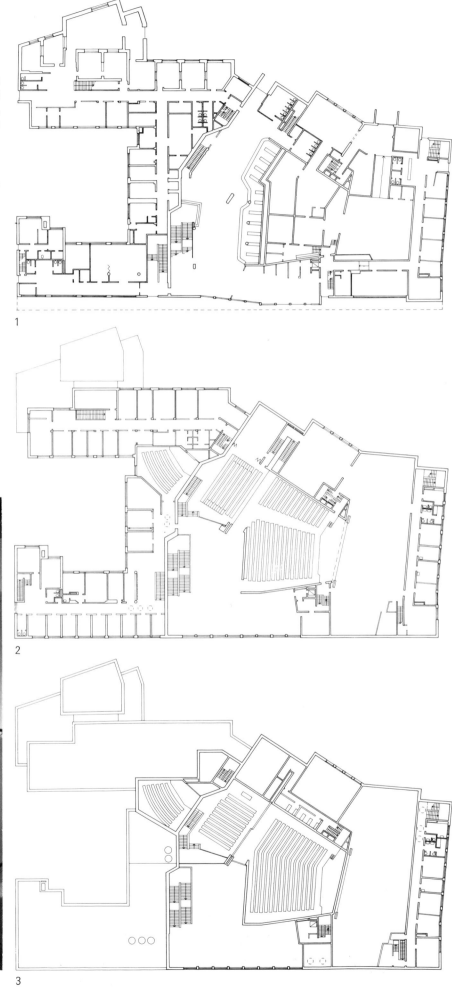

1

2

3

Central Finland Museum
1959 - 1962
Jyväskylä

This museum, built to a tight budget, is to accommodate travelling exhibitions and the Central Finnish Folklore collection. The offices, conference, and work facilities are on the entrance side of the building. A large hall is divided along its length by high clerestory rooflighting, though this is more like a large high window, so that two different kinds of long space are provided in the hall. The lower level is lit by an echelon of circular rooflights, which means that light there falls in pools. This is in contrast to the higher space where all light bounces around off the surfaces. The exterior in its rendered simplicity harks back to Aalto's buildings of the twenties, relying on plays of light on forms for its distinction.

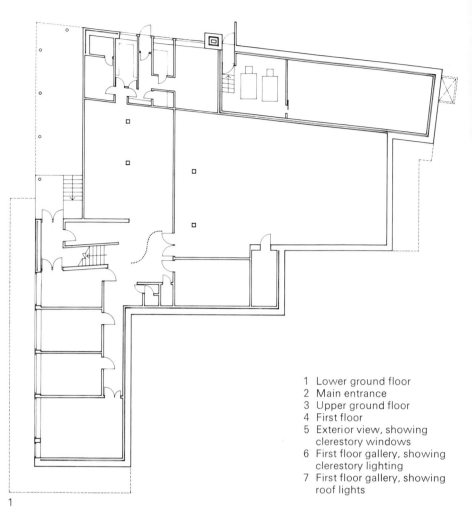

1 Lower ground floor
2 Main entrance
3 Upper ground floor
4 First floor
5 Exterior view, showing
   clerestory windows
6 First floor gallery, showing
   clerestory lighting
7 First floor gallery, showing
   roof lights

1

2

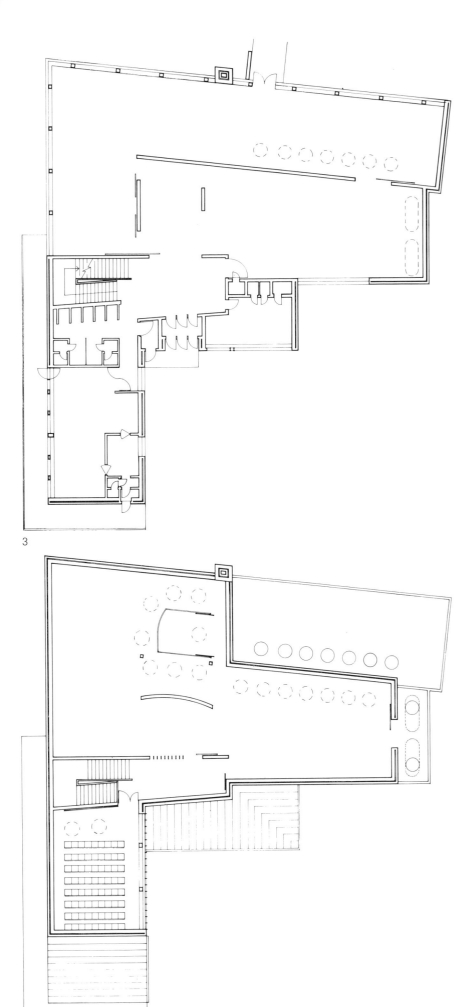

3

4

5

6

7

Town Hall Competition 1949 Completed 1952
Säynätsalo

The original plan for the town centre included a series of blocks stepping away from the town hall. In the event, only the town hall was built, resulting in the absence of the diagonal axis which was to terminate in the council chamber. Nevertheless, Säynätsalo Town Hall has become *the* symptomatic work of Aalto's humanism. There is a mixture of uses in the brief—commercial facilities, offices, council chamber, etc.—which Aalto exploits to the full to produce a building incorporating small-scale elements within an organisation symbolic of the public realm.

This contrast between intimacy and grandeur does much to make the political apparatus of the town appear accessible to the public. For while all the political and bureaucratic functions are grouped around the upper-level courtyard, these functions are housed in volumes which are both introverted around the courtyard and look out over the town.

In the terms mentioned above, it might be interesting to compare the feeling for the importance of the town hall and its public face with Dudok's equally thoughtful town hall at Hilversum.

1

1 General view, showing original grass steps
2 Site plan, showing relationship of proposed housing to town hall
3 Cross section: offices at left; library over shops at right
4 Ground floor
5 First floor, raised courtyard level

2

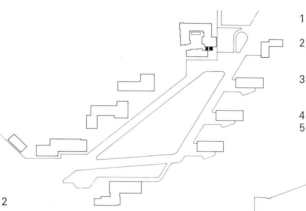

3

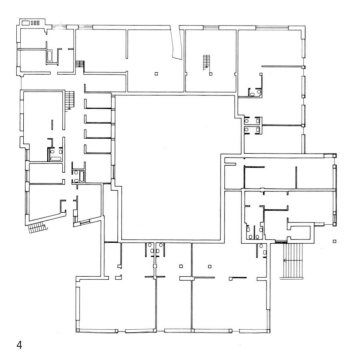

4

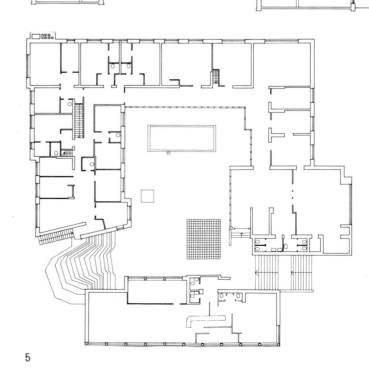

5

6

6 General view
7 Cross section : offices at
  left ; lobby at right, with
  council chamber above
  and clinic below
8 Second floor, council
  chamber level
9 Raised courtyard
10 Roof truss in council
   chamber

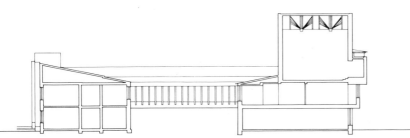

7

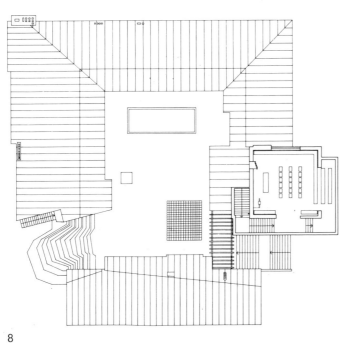

8

9

10

National Pensions Building Competition 1949 Completed 1952
Helsinki

Aalto did not build in Helsinki any building of significance till he was over fifty. This building is one of the first of his large-scale works which, if his town plan for Helsinki ever sees fruition, will add to his architectural domination of that city. Aalto once again had to adapt his prize-winning scheme to a different and more difficult triangular site. Towards the city, the building appears a simple series of blocks 'a redent'. Closer to, the massing breaks down to reveal a courtyard which allows the penetration of sunlight into the depth of the building's mass.

The scale of the building is greatly increased by the horizontal banding of the windows, an expression which speaks of the repetitive nature of the accommodation, but not of the structural frame behind. At ground floor level the familiar sensitivity to the junction between façade and ground is manifested, together with Aalto's mastery of the function of entrance. The stylistic influence of this building is especially noticeable in the English work of Sir Leslie Martin and his assistants.

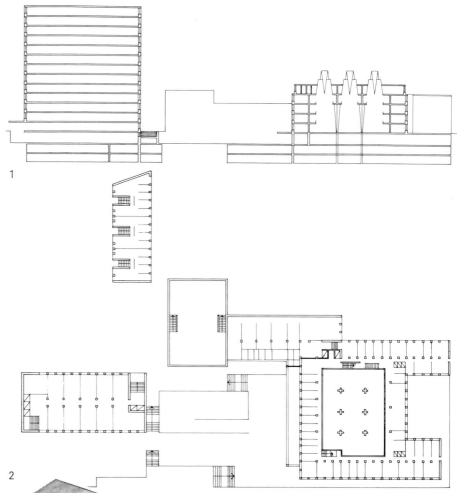

1 Section of competition project
2 Plan of competition project
3 Model of final project

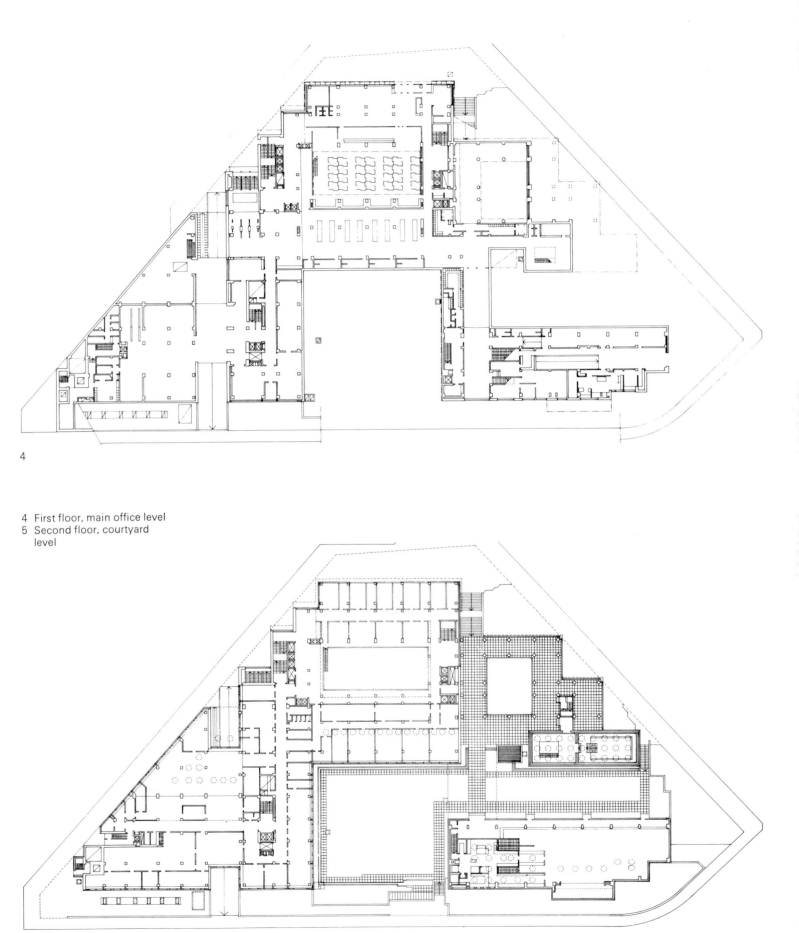

4 First floor, main office level
5 Second floor, courtyard
  level

6

7

6 Library, with large circular
   skylights
7 Main hall from gallery,
   with booths for private
   interviews

Opposite:
General views from the
street

Overleaf:
Detail of windows
Entrance doors and grille
made in bronze with copper-
sheet cladding above and
grey concrete base

Otaniemi Institute of Technology, Main Buildings
Competition 1949
Completion 1964
Otaniemi

The enormous size of this Institute, at least equal to the generation of new 'plate-glass' universities constructed contemporaneously in Great Britain, expanded the size of Aalto's office to such an extent that many of the leading architects of Finland today worked on these buildings.

Dominating the complex is the main auditorium, from which the plan seems to originate. The form of this theatre focusses on the parkland, leaving the enormously high curved brick back wall to address the other buildings. With this gesture of reticent domination, the grid of departments can extend at will through the site, allowing both a grid of covered circulation as well as a large number of points of access. In this aspect, Aalto's plan seems vastly superior to Candilis, Josic and Woods' Free University of Berlin, where a theoretically endless grid admits of no significant points of entry. A plethora of open-sided courtyards bring the surrounding landscape into the buildings.

Perhaps the one criticism that can be levelled at Otaniemi is that the predominant use of one colour of brick is too heavy-handed for a building of this scale, with the result that the applique marble on, for example, the architecture school, seems too trivial a gesture.

1

1 Aerial view
2 Model

Overleaf:
Main auditorium and lecture theatre
General view of main auditorium

Opposite:
Overall view: main auditorium at left; architectural school at right
Library

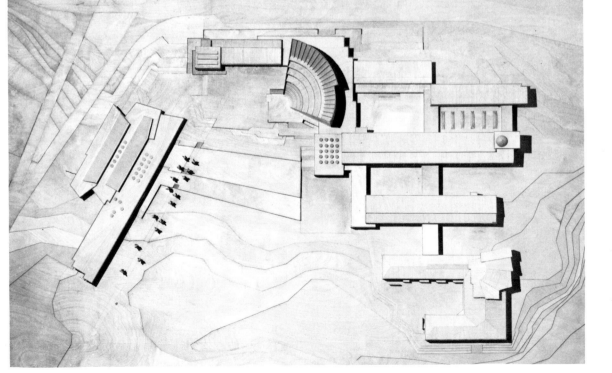

2

87

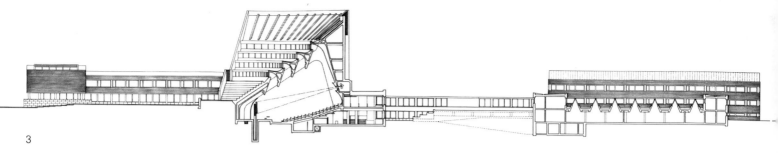

3

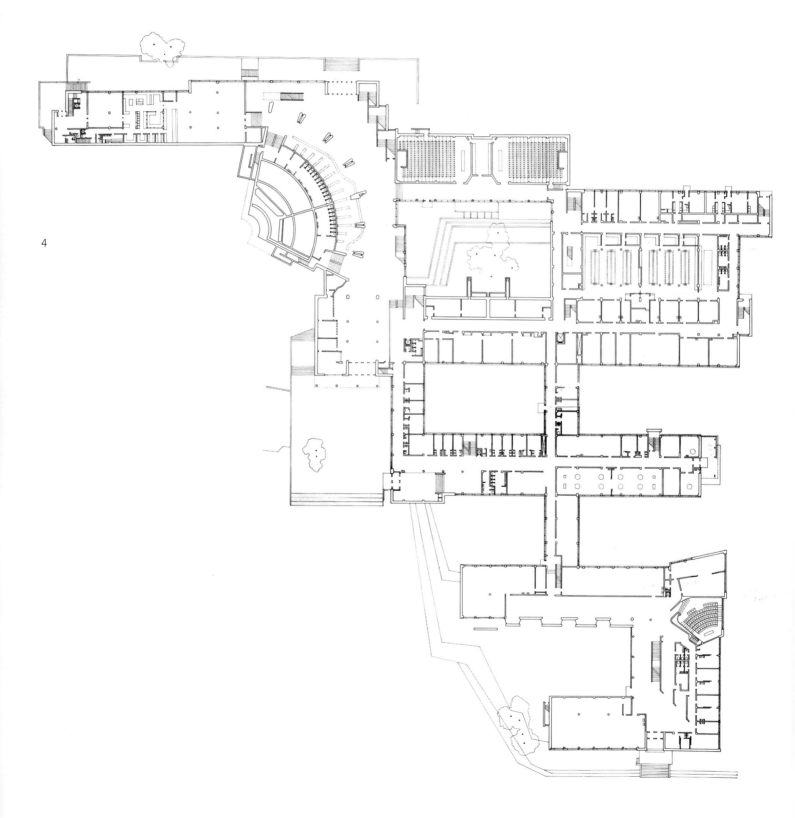

4

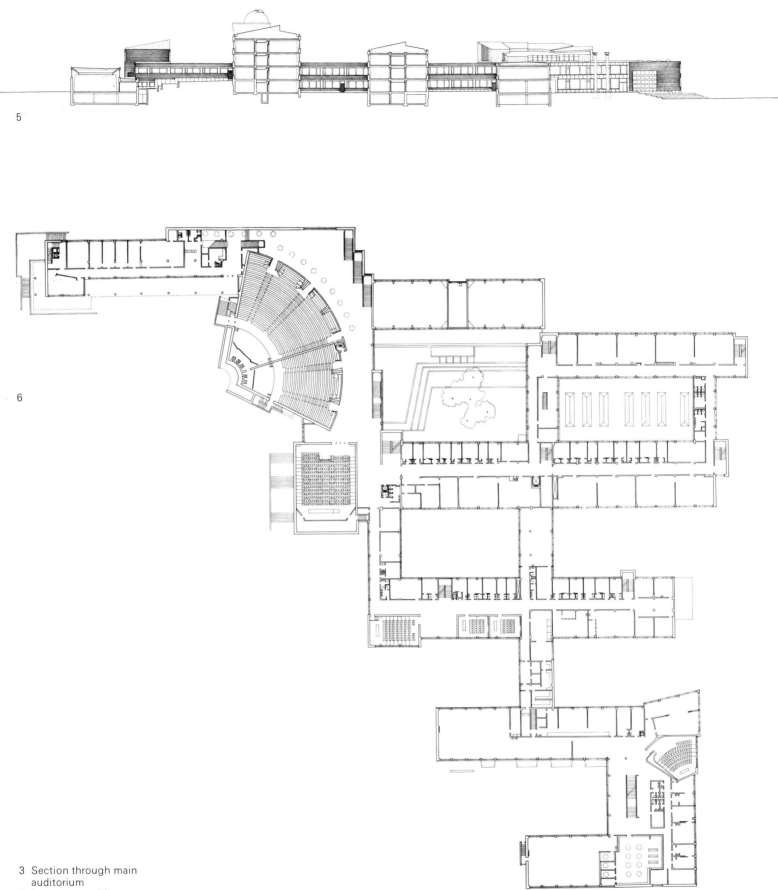

5

6

3 Section through main
   auditorium
4 Lower ground floor
5 Section
6 Upper ground floor

Cultural Centre Competition 1958 Construction 1959 - 1963

Wolfsburg, W. Germany

The building is composed of four elements: a library, a group of hobby rooms, club rooms and meeting rooms, and some communal rooms, and a roof terrace in the centre of the building at first floor level. Externally the horizontally banded walls signify the civic importance, while the *pilotis* demonstrate its openness. In typical Aalto fashion, the centre of the building is a roof terrace, an image of a Greek 'agora' within the privacy of the building, but surely juxtaposed with the town square opposite.

In a sense, this is Aalto at his most abstract: a building constructed around a metaphorical public offering but at the same time making quite clear the conditions of that gift. Despite the impressions given by photographs, the only consistent element, and even that pertains only to the public edges of the building, is the arcade connecting all the many public entrance points.

1

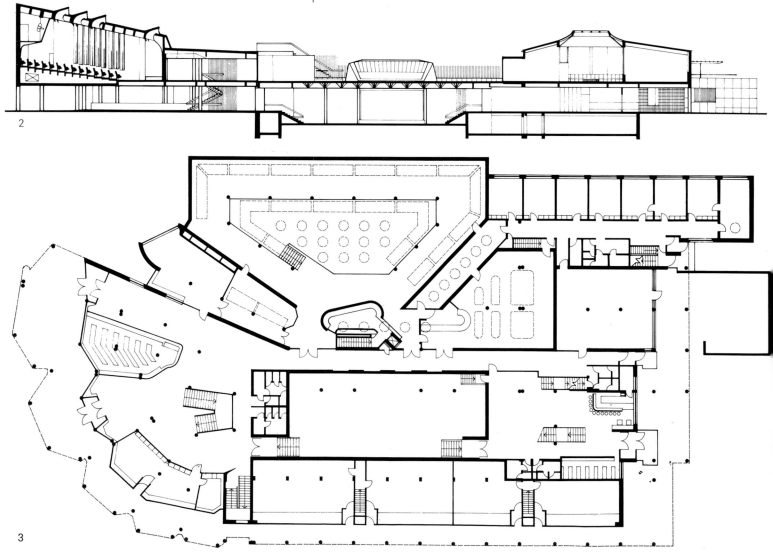

2

3

4

1 Reading room
2 Long section
3 Ground floor
4 View from street
5 First floor, courtyard level

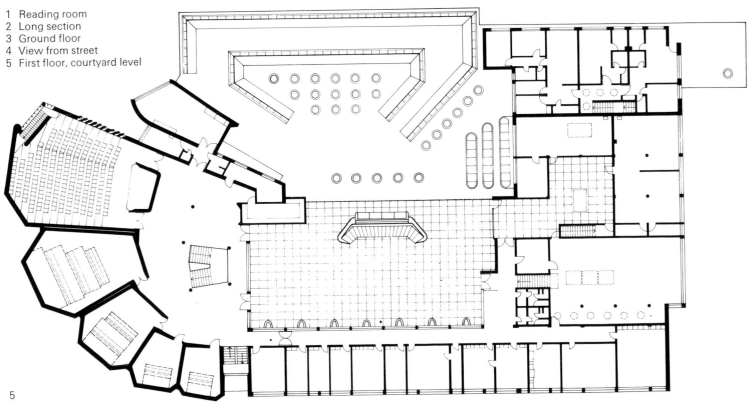

5

Students' Hostel Otaniemi Institute of Technology 1962 - 1966

Otaniemi

This building is composed of four elements : two rectilinear blocks, and a faceted block for accommodation, a courtyard open to the road and the communal facilities, and entrance. At the brow of the hill the two rectilinear blocks form an open courtyard, with the faceted block on the third middle side ; this latter block looks across the contours and down through a wood to the sports facilities.

It is in many ways a very normal building, accepting the repetitiveness of the brief and preserving rhetoric for the entrance and communal facilities and the faceted block by which the scheme is identified from a distance. The organisation of rooms is a model of clarity. Groups of eight to eleven rooms, each with their own shower and WC, are assigned a shared kitchen and lounge. While the scheme is a variant on the three-sided courtyard format, each group of rooms is accessible without impingeing on other groups, thus preserving a civilised degree of privacy within the students' life.

1

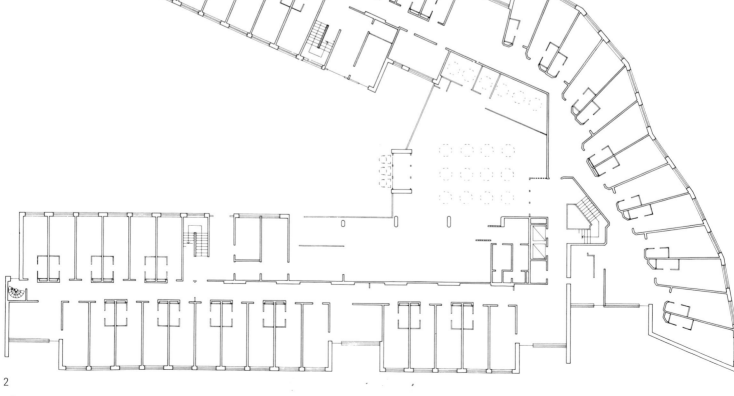

1 General view, showing dormitories
2 Ground floor
3 General view
4 First floor

2

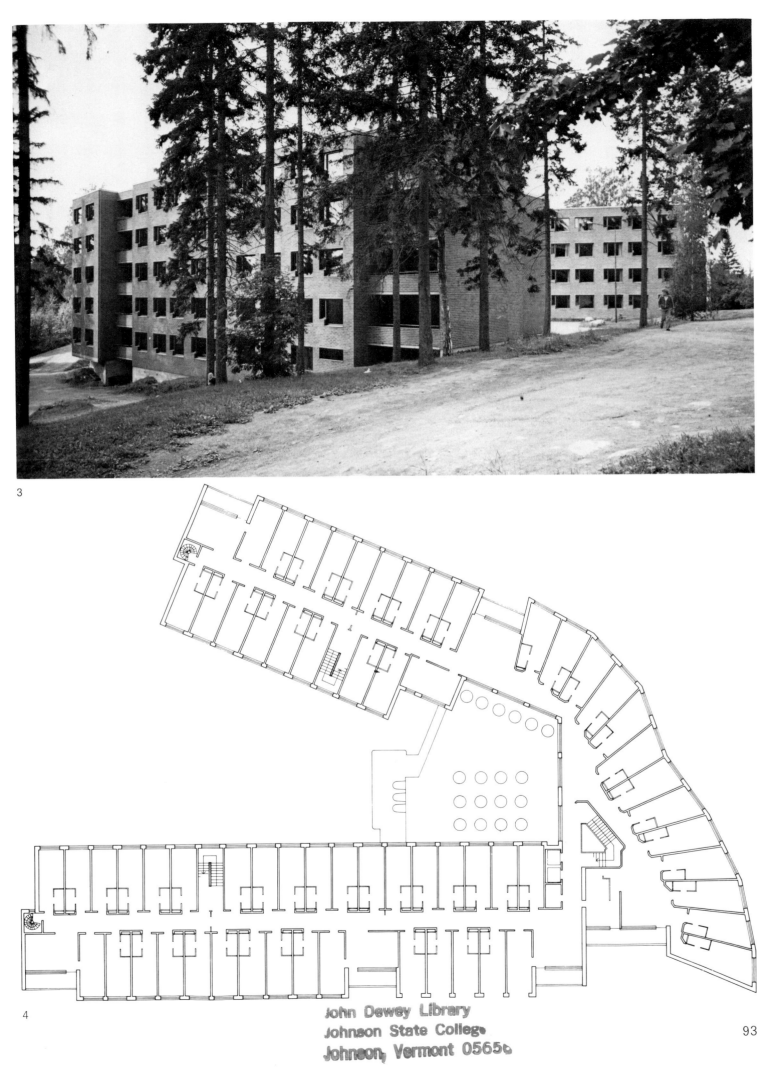

3

4

5

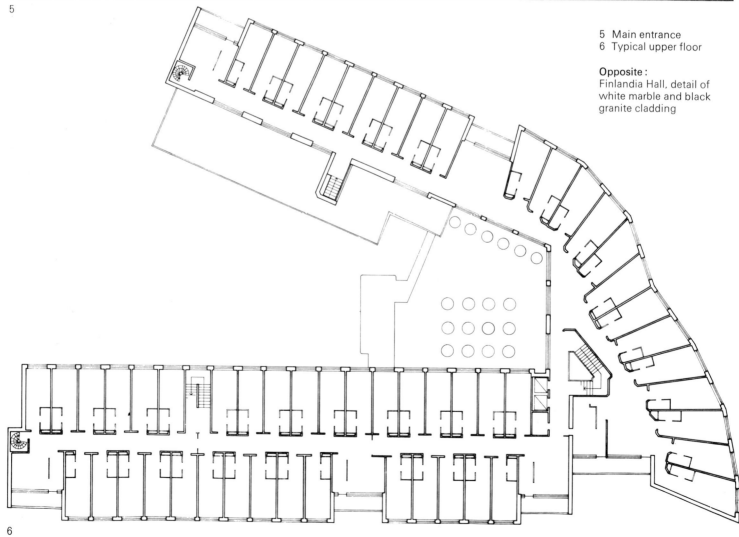

5 Main entrance
6 Typical upper floor

Opposite :
Finlandia Hall, detail of
white marble and black
granite cladding

6

Notes on Responding to Aalto's Buildings
Steven Groak

With the historiographical work of recent scholars, notably those included in this *Architectural Monographs*, it is now becoming possible to chart the various influences in the work of Alvar Aalto and to start to place it in some sort of framework. We may be able to pass beyond the rather vague enthusiasms of even distinguished historians such as Giedion—who at first missed Aalto's significance and then, later, was able only to offer such comments as that the Villa Mairea is 'chamber music'.[1] Just over two years after Aalto's death, though, it is clear that we still lack any satisfactory critical stance on his projects and buildings. Indeed, with the rather incomplete coverage of the only 'authorised version' of published buildings,[2] we lack a proper dossier of the *oeuvre* with which to conduct any extended study: some buildings have been published extensively, but many others have only been seen in the occasional photograph—if at all.

These notes are concerned with three inter-related aspects of the buildings.[3] First of all, and this is a factor rehearsed by earlier authors,[4] there is the dominant role of light in Aalto's work—taken by some to fulfil a harmonising function.[5] Second is the treatment of enclosure and the consequent conception of space embodied in the buildings, which allows discussion of a number of planning elements—the central atrium motif, the functional route, and the nature of the internal and external wall. Thirdly, there is the pervasive use of decoration on all surfaces and, in particular, its role in creating a 'layering' of those surfaces. Together, I would suggest, these allow one to define much of the experience of being and moving in an Aalto building. A wide selection of examples is given—not so much to define an inductive argument, but rather to suggest that Aalto had specific interests early in his career which he evolved and explored over a period of half a century. The sequence therefore signifies the reworking of basic themes already apparent in his earliest work.

Control and Use of Light

There are two key early buildings which illustrate clearly how Aalto used light as a functional determinant of design—the Paimio Sanatorium **7–10** and the Viipuri Library. Both incorporate plan- **11** ning ideas which were developed earlier—and elsewhere[6]—but particularly in the Library can we see the fruits of Aalto's Italian journey of 1924: the part played by strong sunlight in Italian architecture was to have a lasting effect on his work. In a retrospective essay by Aalto, there is a well-known evocation of his design process: *'Whilst designing the library for the town of Viipuri (and I had plenty of time at my disposal—five whole years), I spent a long time making child-like drawings representing an imaginary mountain with different shapes on its sides and, over it, a celestial superstructure crowded with suns which lit the sides with an even light. Visually these drawings had nothing to do with architecture but from their apparent childishness there arose a combination of plans and sections whose inter-weaving it is difficult to know how to describe, and which became the basic concept for the library . . . The concept grouped the reading-rooms, meeting-rooms and the lending library on different levels around the central control—just as the sides of a mountain build up around the ridge. And overhead, a system of suns: the round, conical rooflights of the glazing system.'[7]*

A number of points arise here. First, there is the intention of using architecture to describe the world. Then there is a clearly-implied sequence of spaces, a notion of functional route. And there is, especially, the idea of using light to generate the disposition of those spaces within the building. The Viipuri Library is crucial to the series of libraries in which virtually all of his dominant ideas are completely realised. Apart from the top-lighting conception, and its relation to the routes through the building, there is the exploration of the atrium and the sunken level

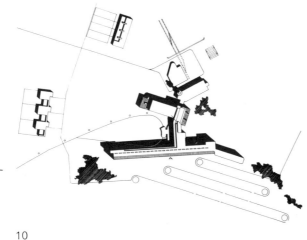

9 10 11

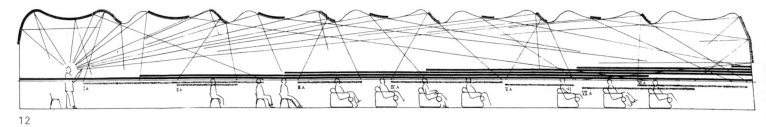

12

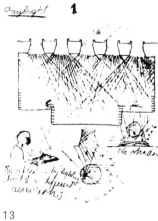

13

14

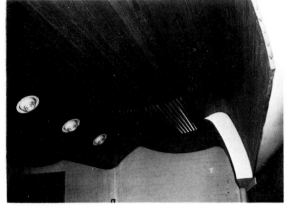

15

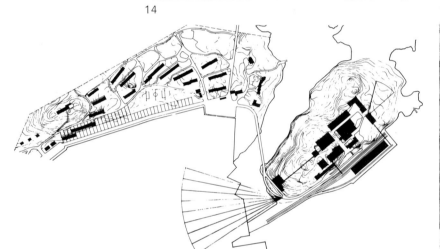

17

18

12 Municipal Library,
   Viipuri : diagram to show
   how sound from the
   speaker will reach any
   part of the lecture room
13 Municipal Library,
   Viipuri : sketch to
   illustrate the principle of
   even light for reading
   (daylight)
14 Cellulose factory, Sunila :
   general view
15 Central Finland Museum,
   Jyväskylä : lecture room
   ceiling
16 Finnish Engineers'
   Institution, Helsinki :
   lecture room ceiling
   detail

19

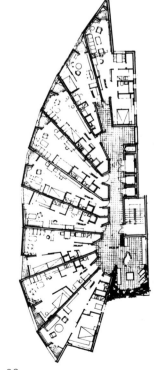

20

21

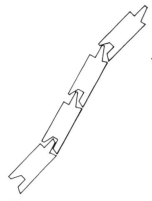

16

17 Cellulose factory, Sunila:
   site plan
18 Rautatalo office building,
   Helsinki: roof lights over
   internal court
19 Neue Vahr apartments,
   Bremen, West Germany:
   general view
20 Neue Vahr apartments,
   Bremen, West Germany:
   typical 'fan' floor plan
21 Furniture: 'fan' corner
   detail
22 Outdoor lighting fitting
23 Door handles
24 Kulttuuritalo, Helsinki:
   general view showing
   auditorium
25 Scandinavia Bank,
   Helsinki: street façade
   with arcade

22

within the atrium. These ideas will be explored further below.

13 The familiar Viipuri diagrams used by Aalto to explain his desire for even lighting in all parts of the reading rooms, are based on the simple geometry of light paths, a technique typical of the period. Interestingly, however, he also used this geometric method to explain a number of other factors: the drawing of the multiple 12 acoustic focii of the lecture room — and the associated physical analogue with a light source — is an obvious example. Similarly, in the Sanatorium he used optical geometry to justify the window system in the wards and to explain the flow of water in the 'non-splash' washbasins. He was to use it again in later works to illustrate acoustic behaviour — for instance, at the church in Imatra and in the concert halls of the Finlandiatalo. But the latter, where acoustic control is of major importance, is a failure, even after attempts to improve the sound in the hall. Despite Aalto's mastery of three-dimensional 'plasticity', it is not clear how far he considered the actual character of sound distribution in a space. Taken with the several examples of undulating reflecting ceilings — apart from Viipuri 15 there are versions at the Central Finland Museum 16 in Jyväskylä, and at the Engineers' Institution in Helsinki — it raises questions about how far Aalto was really concerned with acoustic criteria. (It should be said that this does not mean that such spaces were always acoustic failures, but rather that it may not have been critical.) It may be suggested, then, that at times Aalto was much more interested in certain symbolic characteristics of the spaces involved and that their generation from acoustic requirements was of a questionable nature.

The residual image from these drawings is one from nineteenth- (or even eighteenth-?) century physics: a point source of light radiating straight lines. One is almost tempted to think that the whole set of familiar 'fan' motifs in Aalto's work may derive from this same basic conception — as in the Säynätsalo roof truss, the plan of the Bremen apartment block, the scattered site plan of Sunila, the furniture, and so on. Other examples

include the libraries illustrated elsewhere in this this issue.

Although many, if not most, Aalto buildings appear to exploit the site in the sense of using specific contours, levels, etc., they do not generally provide places from which to view the site and its virtues. Windows for Aalto seem to be devices for bringing light *into* the building, not for giving views to the exterior. Hence, the extensive use of top-lit atria without side views, the rooflight motif, the famous detail of external 2 lamps to rooflights — thus maintaining the character of the light brought into that space, the 18 use of screens over all or part of windows to filter and baffle the light — but which also limit the view, and so on. This preoccupation with mediating the point source of light may be seen in microcosm in the extraordinary number of light fittings that Aalto designed throughout his life. 22 Their range cannot be explained by the argument that he simply designed special light fittings for each building, because he was prepared to use a very limited range of furniture and door handles in those same buildings. 23

The final point to be made here is one concerning light and reflecting surfaces. It appears in virtually all of Aalto's buildings that, where a wall has no openings, one of two things is happening: either there is a staircase on the other side, or the wall is a reflector for sound or light. That is, one may read off the exterior an indication of the function — for instance, an auditorium or a rooflit 24 enclosure — without having to see people using the building. This must lead on to a discussion of Aalto's conception of space and how it is defined by walls and enclosure.

Enclosure and Space
In his treatment of enclosure and space, Aalto provides many puzzles for anyone versed in the disciplines of the Modern Movement. First of all, there is in his buildings a clear differentiation between inside and outside. Not for Aalto the continuum of internal and external space. This may be seen clearly in his urban buildings: with the minor exception of the Scandinavian Bank in 25 Helsinki, these are always built up to the street

23   24   25

26 boundary. The main façade is as it were a 'hard face' actively to be penetrated. This characteristic may be seen in his early buildings – for instance, the Labour Club and the Civil Guard **27** building (now the Post Office) in Jyväskylä, or **28** the Turun Sanomat and Standard Apartments in Turku. Secondly, although he is well prepared to exploit the grid in three dimensions – eg. the **32** Enso-Gutzeit building in Helsinki – it is in his ability to counterpoint with non-grid elements or to 'disjoint' the grid that Aalto achieves some of his most powerful expression. This may be seen in the bifurcated plan of the Kulttuuritalo, in the **33** Villa Mairea, in the Otaniemi main building, in **36** the plan of Muuratsalo, in the Hansaviertel block **34** in Berlin, in the Alajärvi Town Hall, in the housing **35** at Sunila, and in the whole range of town centre plans he produced over the years.

With this distinction between interior and exterior, the route takes on great importance, especially in the public buildings. (Indeed, it may be that the relative unimportance (?) of routing in the private house diminished Aalto's interest in the house as a design problem, for it must be admitted that this type does seem the weakest area of his work – his houses do not begin to compare, for instance, with those of Frank Lloyd Wright or Le Corbusier, except in his impressive control of their public domain.) Typically, one enters Aalto's public buildings through any of a number of entrances, perhaps at varying levels. There is then some change of level or transitional space to translate the audience to the next space – usually an antechamber or lounge. From here one's subsequent route – eg. to enter the concert auditorium in due course – may be surveyed at leisure. The process of leaving the building is cared for with equal felicity. There is a sequence of surprises, but not ones which disorientate. The route is marked as it unravels; externally, there are sufficient clues – visible from many angles – to indicate major elements and relationships. In some buildings, **37** such as Baker House at MIT, the route itself is labelled on the outside of the building. It does appear that Aalto's buildings are not only some of the most spatially-complex devised, they are also amongst the easiest in which to organise

oneself and to find one's way.

Considered as a type, the libraries illustrate another feature, namely Aalto's interest in mixing rectilinear and free forms within one building. The route is then announced at the junction (or disjunction?) of these forms. This complexity appears in early buildings – eg. the main entrance to the Paimio Sanatorium, repeated in the Otaniemi Student Hostel. Some observers have taken this to be a sign of Aalto's organic approach to building synthesis.[8] But the forms themselves represent functions in the sense that different forms announce different internal uses and scales of internal organisation.

Following his visit to Italy in 1924, Aalto became fascinated by the classical atrium.[9] The idea is clearly expressed in the early study for his brother's house – the Casa Väinö Aalto – although not included in the eventual building. It remains in later works such as the somewhat curious building for the City Electricity Company **41** in Helsinki. The atrium – the cutting away of the central volume – becomes a major feature of Aalto's buildings. By 'hollowing out' and stepping the residual solid, Aalto creates a multiplicity of surfaces through which light may be brought into the building. This may be strongly **40** contrasted with the 'hard face' on the main façade mentioned above, in the case of urban infill buildings. In a number of buildings, the atrium motif is elaborated by culminating in a toplit internal hall. (Within several of these 'be- **38** hind-the-scene' spaces may be found a strange reference to traditional Finnish military architecture in the form of turret staircases – eg. Turun **29** Sanomat, City Electricity Company, Jyväskylä **36** Post Office – and has echoes in the National Pensions Employees' housing in Helsinki.)

I would suggest that Aalto's use of the atrium, present throughout his career, is associated with his preoccupation with light and, in particular, with the path of the sun around the building. The cutaway volume creates a richness and system of light sources central to his architectural concern. Baird[10] has suggested that this physical feature of the buildings, when combined with the in-

26 Rautatalo office building, Helsinki : general view, showing façade built up to boundary
27 Civil Guards Building (now Post Office), Jyväskylä : general view, showing building up to street boundary
28 Turun Sanomat building, Turku : general view, showing façade built up to boundary
29 Turun Sanomat building, Turku : off-street courtyard showing turret staircase
30 City Electricity Company, Helsinki : view over top of the roof lights to banking hall, showing turret staircase
31 Hansaviertel apartments, West Berlin : typical floor plan showing distension of the planning grid

31

26

27

28

29

30

32 Enso-Gutzeit building, Helsinki : general view showing three-dimensional grid, with break to allow vehicle entrance
33 Villa Mairea, Noormarku : general view showing curved balcony against rectilinear massing
34 Terrace housing for supervisory staff, Sunila : typical floor plan showing distension of the planning grid
35 Terrace housing for factory staff, Sunila
36 Hansaviertel apartments, West Berlin

32

33

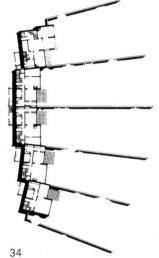

34

35

36

37 Baker House, MIT Senior Dormitory, Cambridge, USA : general view showing the expression of the staircase route
38 City Electricity Company, Helsinki : aerial view showing central 'atrium'
39 Apartments for National Pensions staff, Helsinki : view of staircase
40 Enso-Gutzeit building, Helsinki : rear elevation, showing cutaway volume and system of 'screens'
41 City Electricity Company, Helsinki : toplit internal 'atrium' of banking hall

37

38

39

40

41

creased use of greenery, constitutes an 'instant ruin': he proposes that Aalto was worried about the relics he would leave to posterity and that he attempted to pre-empt the ravages of time and weather. Another view may be considered. It was suggested above that throughout his career Aalto transformed a set of early ideas, so that the themes inform the sequence of buildings. For this reason, I would further suggest, that in a sense Aalto did not complete his buildings, and the apparently arbitrary 'hollowing out' of the primary volume is one expression of that idea. We know that Aalto was forever redesigning schemes, refining ideas through competition schemes,[11] and this seems to be both part of his work pattern and part of the puzzle we experience in trying to apprehend the buildings.

This interpretation goes some way to explicate the familiar system of devices, amongst which is Aalto's use of the screen. It can be seen in the treatment of the atrium of the Paris Expo building (1937) and the project for the Finnish Embassy in Moscow (1935). He uses virtually every building material — timber, copper, ceramic tiles, terra-cotta, marble, etc. — at some time or other **42-50** to create these screens, which occur both internally and externally. Two important characteristics should be noted: first, the screens are usually vertical; secondly, they are usually flush with the surrounding wall surface, unless they are part of a superimposed decoration. Consequently, various openings in the wall behind the screen(s) are successively revealed and hidden as the observer moves around the building or as the sun passes around the building. (The screen element would generally read more distinctly if proud or recessed — this does occasionally occur, **52** such as on the Central Finland Museum in Jyväskylä.) On occasion the screen blends with the wall treatment, such that it becomes very **53** difficult to define where solid changes to void. On other occasions, this is accomplished by continuing the wall decoration across the opening. **51** This appears to be part of a process of 'layering' of the surface, a use of decoration which is peculiarly Aalto's. For some it may be that this camouflage of the formal order is, in a sense, cheating on the tenets of modern functionalist

approaches. However, from the point of view of the conception of space entailed, I would suggest that it constitutes a 'dematerialisation' of the wall as an element.

Mosso[12] has suggested that these screens or 'meshes' allow the internal and external spaces to 'breathe' through the wall. However, it seems to me that the effect one experiences is *not* to lose the wall's function as a definition or partition of space in the traditional proposition of the Modern Movement, because each space continues to be read separately. For me, this point is emphasised by the evocative soft-pencil sketches prepared by Aalto for many of his schemes, wherein internal or external spaces are drawn quite distinctly from each other. Were they to be read as a continuum, it could well be that this would diminish the significance of the route as a primary element in Aalto's scheme of things.

Subsidiary versions of the 'dematerialising' function of screens also exist. The treatment of doors in some cases transforms them into elaborations or continuations of a screen. And, on occasions — eg. the undulating ceilings discussed above — the junction between wall and ceiling within a room is such as to lose the corner by taking the wall past the plane of the ceiling.

If it is accepted that Aalto seeks at times to 'dematerialise' the enclosure and, moreover, that unbroken surfaces denote hidden reflectance or vertical movement, then it is possible to go further in discussing the organisation of many of his buildings. I would propose that the buildings be seen as objects at the intersection of two routes — that of the sun around the building and that of the observer following some path around and through the building. (And on occasion the built form is partially generated as a 'fan', with consequent significance given to its origin.) In this sense, all walls and surfaces serve simultaneously to control, baffle or redistribute the light coming into or onto the building and to mark the various routes. It is not coincidence but indeed almost a property of this proposal, then, that many of the buildings have several entrances. Moreover, if we observe that in many instances — but especi-

42 Finlandiatalo, Helsinki: view of window to Convention Hall, showing 'screens'
43 Finlandiatalo, Helsinki: general view of lounge area of main concert hall, showing stairs on external wall and 'screen detail to balcony
44 Library, Institute of Technology, Otaniemi: view of front entrance, showing terra-cotta screen over window

42

43

44

45

46

45 Municipal Library, Seinäjoki : general view, showing screening of windows looking onto central area

46 Villa Carré, Bazoches, France : side elevation, showing painted brickwork and screening of window

47 Town Hall, Säynätsalo : general view, showing screening of upper windows (Library) etc.

48 Alvar Aalto Museum, Jyväskylä : general view, showing roof lights and tiling to walls passing over windows

49 Kulttuuritalo, Helsinki : detail of 'screen' door and corrugated copper cladding

50 Church, Seinäjoki : detail of interior screen

51 Town Hall, Seinäjoki : detail of window with half-round tiled surface carried across mullions, forming 'screen' and layering surface

52 Central Finland Museum, Jyväskylä : view of entrance, showing screen to lecture room window with screen proud of wall

53 Municipal Library, Rovaniemi : view of entrance, showing clerestory, tiled walls and screened window

47

48

49

50

51

52

53

103

ally in the medium/large public buildings — a functional change in the route is distinguished by a change in level, then it becomes very important how and where stairs are placed. In his RIBA Gold Medal address, Aalto recounted: *'Once I tried to make a standardisation of staircases. Probably that is one of the oldest of the standardisations. Of course, we design new staircase steps every day . . . We tried to solve the matter by an elastic system . . . For the movement of the human being there is a special rhythmical form. You can't make a step how you like; it must be a special proportion. I spoke about that in the University at Gothenburg. The Rector . . . came out with a book – Dante's* Divine Comedy. *He opened it at the page where it says that the worst thing in the* Inferno *is that the stairs had the wrong proportions.'*[13]

The stairs in Aalto's plans express the richness described for the routing system. Their complexities — sometimes moving away from rectilinearity, sometimes being subdivided or masked by rails (screens?) in various subtle ways — and, on occasion, their apparent overprovision, all point to their importance as guiding elements in deciphering the building as one moves through and around.

This series of relationships and, in effect, corollaries perhaps begins to contrast with those rather impressionistic effusions that would place Aalto's work as some simple organic response to the Finnish countryside, a stance rightly castigated by Mosso.[14] It is argued that the work comprises a highly-ordered development, albeit of a very individual kind. The means of defining and denoting space may now be examined further in the context of Aalto's extensive use of decorative forms.

The Use of Decoration

Aalto used decoration throughout his career, eschewing it only perhaps in those few buildings which place him firmly in the Functionalist camp — the Paimio Sanatorium, the Turun Sanomat, the Standard Apartments in Turku, etc. Maxwell[15] has suggested that in Aalto the function of decoration is, as it were, to dress the buildings in conventional clothes to make them acceptable at an everyday level. This does presuppose that the underlying forms are somehow strange. Porphyrios[16] has mentioned that in all Aalto's decorative work there is an acceptance of the Byzantine tradition of *bricolage*, of the ability to employ any materials to achieve a desired effect.

The decoration is usually related to the buildings and their form, it is not whimsical. Sometimes it exploits the intrinsic characteristics of the materials used in constructing the walls and enclosure — their colour or texture. (Mosso[17] has noted that Aalto rarely adds colour as a finish.) Sometimes the decoration is laid across both surface and opening — as discussed above in the use of screens. It is often used to express a layering of planes within a wall — again, this may be related to the proposal that he will seek to dematerialise the solidity of the enclosure without necessarily opening up the space defined. The most complex example that springs to mind is the Town Hall at Seinäjoki, with its ordering of blue tiles, white stucco, glass and timber above a grey granite 'ground course'. The system of layering and baffling of light is carried throughout the building — eg. the entrance and council chamber.

Another dominant form of decoration used by Aalto is the 'corduroy' effect of half-round ceramic tiles hung vertically in panels, as in the Rovaniemi Library. It has echoes in the corrugated copper sheeting used in the National Pensions building, the City Electricity building and the Kulttuuritalo. The tile system will sometimes drape the surface, terminating in an apparently arbitrary pattern, such as in the Alvar Aalto Museum at Jyväskylä. The detail appears to refer to the traditional timber cladding of butt-jointed boards with narrow cover pieces which Aalto used in his earliest buildings — eg. the Two-family House in Jyväskylä, the Villa Väinölä and the Hospital and Youth Society buildings in Alajärvi. This vertical timber detail reappears in the famous timber walls of the 1930s — Aalto's own house, the Villa Mairea, the Finnish Pavilions for the 1937 Paris Expo and the 1939 New York World's Fair, and for a whole

54   55   56   57   58

59 Municipal Library, Rovaniemi : exterior of reading room, showing 'corduroy' effect of tiling, and internal reflecting surfaces to clerestory window

60 City Electricity Company, Helsinki : detail showing corrugated copper cladding

61 Alvar Aalto Museum, Jyväskylä : view of roof light and surface, with flat and half-round tiles giving 'corduroy' effect

62 Two-family house, Jyväskylä : general view, showing new timber cladding and altered staircase, and 'corduroy' surface effect

63 Finnish pavilion, Paris Expo 1937 : detail of timber cladding

64 Hospital, Alajärvi : general view, showing colonnade and timber cladding

65 Architect's house, Helsinki : general view, showing timber cladding

66 Finnish Pavilion, New York World's Fair 1939 : undulating timber wall of interior

67 Finnish Pavilion, Paris Expo : view of entrance, showing timber cladding

68 Villa Mairea, Noormarku : detail of timber cladding

59

60

61

62

63

64

65

66

67

68

range of industrial buildings, such as the factory
69 at Karhula. The motif remains even in late work —
1 eg. the gallery of the Alvar Aalto Museum. (The
link is also to the undulating ceilings discussed
above, in the context of light and sound.) One
can see in a late building like the Lappia House,
with its surface of various tiles, how the appearance of the building changes with the direc-
3,4 tion and colour of natural light: the layering of
the surface — and hence its 'materialisation' —
adjusts with the light. The change is so specific
and related to the movement of light that one
cannot consider it as accidental in the work of a
designer of Aalto's sensitivity.

Small-scale decoration was also part of Aalto's
design vocabulary from his earliest neo-classical
buildings, and was part of their delicacy — eg. the
70 Apartment Block for railway workers at Jyväs-
71 kylä, on the corbels to the Civil Guard building at
73 Seinäjoki, in the frieze to the Post Office at
Jyväskylä and so on. (There are less successful
examples, such as the sculpture on the office
74 building at Rovaniemi.)

From the 1930s onwards, Aalto appears in-
creasingly to have sought the decorative pos-
sibilities of materials 'in themselves'. The
75 experimental wall at Muuratsalo is well known.
76 The Otaniemi Power House at times reads almost
as an attempt to evoke the scale of solid versus
glass of the Paimio Sanatorium, but for me the
red brick does not quite relate to the scale of the
panels it comprises — a difficulty also experienced
with the lecture hall of the main building in that
complex. His use of white marble is of interest.
It is used at Otaniemi essentially as marker — it
identifies the entrance to the Library and, across
the park, forms an appliqué façade to the
72 Architecture School in a way that is surely a
deliberate joke, referring to the past. His detailing
77 of the marble cladding to the Enso-Gutzeit
building in Helsinki, however, is unsatisfactory.
But the exploration of marble surfaces in the
Finlandiatalo seems to me totally successful. Not
43 only is it used both as screen, located by stairs
78 behind and in front, and as reflecting surface, it
79 also allows one to realise that Aalto conceived
of the building being seen at many different

times of the day and the year. The marble on
Finlandiatalo takes on quite different colour and
texture as the light alters.
5,6

Aalto used white stucco on and off throughout
his work — eg. the inner courtyard of the South- **81**
West Finnish Farmers' Cooperative in Turku, the **82**
Paimio Sanatorium, and more recently the
Apartment Block and the Central Finland **83**
Museum at Jyväskylä. He is also prepared to **84**
paint external brickwork white — eg. Villa Carré **46**
in France and the Korkalovaara housing at **85**
Rovaniemi. But he did not for long accept the **87**
white wall aesthetic which dominated the
Modern Movement. Insofar as he explored ideas
of the 'hole-in-the-wall' treatment of the elevation, it appears much more in intrinsically solid
materials such as brick — eg. in the residential
blocks at Jyväskylä University or the Otaniemi **88**
Student Hostel. And even then these materials **86**
may be given some 'dematerialising' aspect, such
as the 'crenellations' at Säynätsalo — a detail
which harks back to the butt-jointed timber
cladding discussed above. **80**

A final detail worth mentioning here is that by
which Aalto's buildings meet the ground. Time
and again, he will create a stepped detail as the
wall material is unravelled against the ground
line — perhaps running above a granite base.
Since the degree of stepping involved is unlikely
to occur on the floor inside the wall, and the
fenestration will often give the clue here, the
decorative device suggests that what may be a
solid material — eg. red brick — is not entirely
load-bearing, that on the exterior it is essentially
a decorative surface. Once again, the solidity of
the wall is denied by the surface treatment.

Conclusion
Aalto works with light, with the route, with massing and modelling of the building form. These
are classic architectural references. His range is
formidable in that he appears able to handle an
extraordinarily wide spectrum of architectural
problems. He handles the urban and the rural,
the large, medium and small building. He is able
to absorb virtually every building material, be it
concrete and stucco, glass, copper, marble

69 Pulp mill, Karhula: detail
of timber cladding
70 Railway workers'
apartments, Jyväskylä:
general view
71 Railway workers'
apartments, Jyväskylä:
detail of doors to main
stairs — at the back of the
building

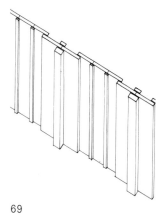

69

70

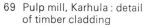

71

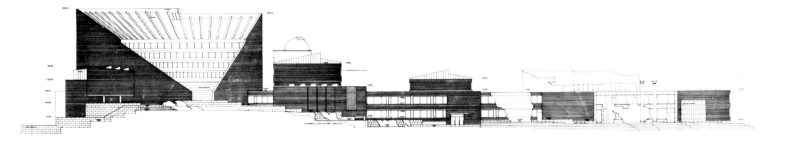

72

72 Main Building, Institute of Technology, Otaniemi: elevation showing white marble classical references of façade treatment to architecture school

73 Civil Guard Headquarters, Seinäjoki: general view, showing decorative detail such as painted corbels

74 Commercial/residential building, Rovaniemi: general view, showing Aalto sculpture on the side of the building

75 Summer house, Muuratsalo: view of courtyard with brick and ceramic experiments

76 Power House, Institute of Technology, Otaniemi: general view

77 Enso-Gutzeit building, Helsinki: detail of marble cladding which is showing signs of cracking

78 Finlandiatalo, Helsinki: elevation of lounge to main concert hall, showing marble 'screen', defined by stairs behind and in front of its plane

79 Finlandiatalo, Helsinki: view of exterior of main concert hall, showing detail of white marble and dark grey granite

73

74

75

76

77

78

79

brick, ceramics or timber. Within this vocabulary, his designs exhibit a formal order and systematic approaches, transformed and developed throughout his career.

Aalto is clearly preoccupied with the control of light and relates it very strongly to the possible routes around and within a building : there is a clear invitation to decipher the building externally before exploring the interior, even though he always remains slightly guarded. For this reason too, perhaps, there is a clear separation between inside and outside. Mosso[18] has made much of Aalto's melding light into space to create a unique 'plastic' whole. However, it is not clear what formal significance he sees this contributing to the buildings. It has been argued here that the preoccupation with light is actually a generative source of Aalto's highly individual conception of space and enclosure.

Aalto's buildings, for me, exist as objects which combine systems of activity routes for people and the system of possible light sources. The use of decoration is then part of a complex means by which wall elements in particular are 'dematerialised' in order to symbolise this penetration and combination. Beyond this approach — and Benevolo[19] for one has argued a concern with typology as quintessentially Aalto — he rests within the set of traditions identified by Pearson, Heinonen, Porphyrios, and others. Aalto's use of space appears 'loose' at its edges, but the defining/enclosing building is never really transparent. He remains strange but perhaps not mysterious : there is much concern to give the user clues to the building.

The historiographical account should soon be sufficiently established for an adequate theoretic approach — one concerned with interpretation rather than intention — to become possible. How this will emerge remains to be seen, but whichever form it takes it must surely refer to the experience of the buildings themselves.

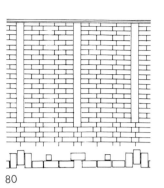

80

80 Town Centre, Säynätsalo : detail of external brickwork, which appears to relate to early timber butt-jointed cladding
81 South-West Finnish Farmers' Cooperative, Turku : view of central courtyard — white/cream stucco
82 South-West Finnish Farmers' Cooperative, Turku : general view
83 High-rise apartments, Jyväskylä : general view
84 Central Finland Museum, Jyväskylä : general view, showing use of white stucco
85 Korkalovaara housing, Rovaniemi : general view of apartment block
86 Student Hostel, Institute of Technology, Otaniemi : elevation showing typical 'hole-in-wall' window detail
87 Korkalovaara housing, Rovaniemi : part of typical terrace housing
88 Pedagogical University, Jyväskylä : elevation of residential building showing typical 'hole-in-wall' window detail

Notes

1 S. Giedion, *Space, Time and Architecture*, 3rd edition, Harvard University Press, Cambridge, Mass., 1954, p. 592.

2 K. Fleig (ed.), *Alvar Aalto I. 1922–62*. Verlag für Architektur Artemis, Zürich, 1963 ; *Alvar Aalto II, 1963–70*, Verlag für Architektur Artemis, Zürich, 1971.

3 I am indebted to David Dunster and to Nadir Tharani for many helpful comments during the preparation of this article.

4 eg. L. Mosso, 'La luce nell'architettura di Alvar Aalto', *Zodiac*, No. 7, 1960, pp. 67–115.

5 eg. R. Maxwell, 'The Venturi Effect', *Architectural Monographs*, No. 1, 1978, p. 26.

6 P. D. Pearson, *Alvar Aalto and the International Style*, Whitney Library of Design, New York, 1978, p. 85, p. 112.

7 A. Aalto, 'The Egg of the Fish and the Salmon', *Architects' Year Book*, No. 8, Elek Books, London, 1957, p. 138.

8 eg. Testimonial by C. Norberg-Schulz in Memorial Issue of *Arkkitehti*, July–August 1976, p. 51.

9 Pearson, *op.cit.*, p. 43.

10 G. Baird and Y. Futogawa, *Alvar Aalto*, Thames & Hudson, London, 1970, pp. 11–14.

11 Pearson, *op.cit.*, p. 59.

12 Mosso, *op.cit.*, p. 80.

13 A. Aalto, 'RIBA Annual Discourse', *Architects' Year Book*, No. 8, Elek Books, London, 1957, p. 142 ; *RIBA Journal*, May, 1957.

14 L. Mosso, 'Introduction', *L'Architecture d'Aujourd'hui*, No. 191, June 1977, p. 57.

15 Maxwell, *loc.cit.*

16 Personal communication.

17 L. Mosso, *Zodiac, op.cit.*, p. 87.

18 Mosso, *op.cit.*

19 L. Benevolo, *History of Modern Architecture, Volume 2: The modern movement*, Routledge & Kegan Paul, London, 1971, p. 704.

81

82

83

84

85

86

87

88

Alvar Aalto: List of Buildings and Projects

(This list has been compiled from various sources, and while not claiming to be complete, is believed to be the most up-to-date list currently available. Dates given are those of completion of the building.)

1898   Born 3rd May

1918   Renovation of parents' house, Alajärvi

1918 (?) Entrance to shopping co-operative, Alajärvi (demolished)

1919-20 Youth Society Building, Alajärvi (became Civil Guards Building)

1920   Monument to the Dead of the Civil War, Alajärvi

1920   Tivoli area of the Finnish National Fair, Helsinki (assisting Carolus Lindberg)

1921-23 Church and belfry, Kauhajärvi

1922   Industrial Exhibition, Tampere

1923 (?) House, 'Nuora', Jyväskylä

1923   Parliament site plan, Helsinki : competition entry

1924   Parliament House, Helsinki : competition entry

1924-25 Apartment building, Jyväskylä

1924-25 Workers' Club, Jyväskylä

c. 1925 Summer house, Karstula

1925   Church, Jämsä : competition entry

1925   Church renovation, Viitasaari

1925   Casa Laurén, two-family house, Jyväskylä

1925   Civil Guard Buildings, Seinäjoki

c. 1926 Villa Väinölä, Alajärvi

1926   Union Bank Headquarters and Office Building, Helsinki : competition entry

1926   Villa Flora, Alajärvi, architect Aino Aalto

1926-27 League of Nations, Geneva : competition entry

1927   Töölö church, Helsinki : competition entry

1927   Municipal Hospital, Alajärvi

1927   Church renovation, Pylkönmäki

1927   Viinikka church, Tampere : competition entry

1927   Taulmäki church, Jyväskyla : competition entry

1927   Office block, Vaasa : competition entry (with E. Bryggman)

1927-29 Building for the Civil Guard 'Keski-Suomen Suoja Oy', Jyväskylä (1926 competition entry won second prize ; the building later became the Post Office)

1928   South-western Agricultural Co-operative building, Turku (competition held in 1926)

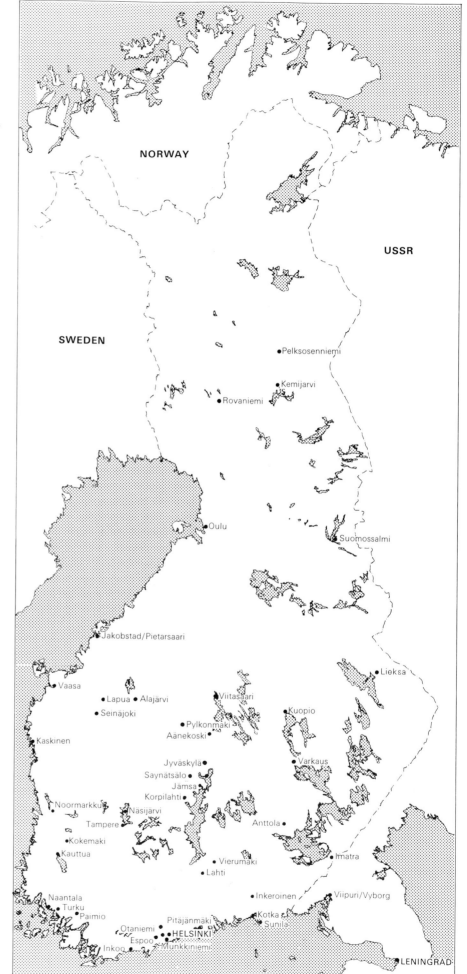

1928	AITTA competition entries for summer houses
1928	Church renovation, Korpilahti
1928	Finnish Independence Monument, Helsinki : competition entry
1928–30	Turun Sanomat newspaper building, Turku
1929	Church, Muurame
1929	Apartment building, Turku
1929	Columbus Lighthouse, Santo Domingo, Dominican Republic : competition entry
1929	Church renovation, Kemijärvi
1929	Turku 700th centenary exhibition (with E. Bryggman)
1929	Bandstand, Turku 700th centenary exhibition
1929	Wooden stacking chairs
1929	Thonet-Mundus International chair competition entry, Vienna
1930	Water tower, Turku : competition entry
1930	Tehtaanpuisto Mikael Agricola church, Helsinki : competition entry
1930	Grave of Usko Nyström, Helsinki
1930	Sports Institute, Vierumäki : competition entry, 3rd prize
1930	Apartment and Housing Exhibition material for CIAM conference, Brussels
1930	Exhibition : The Minimum Apartment, Helsinki
1930	'S.O.S.' stage sets, Turku

Youth Society Building, Alajärvi, 1919–20

Casa Laurén, Jyväskylä, 1925. Photo Keski-Suomen Museo

Helsinki area, showing location of buildings by Alvar Aalto

1 Villa Aalto
   Riihitie 20, Munkkiniemi
2 Savoy restaurant (interior)
   E. Esplanadikatu 14
3 Block of flats for employees of the National Pensions Institute
   Riihitie 12–14, Munkkiniemi
4 Rautatalo (Iron House)
   Keskuskatu 3
5 National Pensions Institute
   Minna Canthinkatu 15
6 Architect's studio
   Tiilimäki 20, Munkkiniemi
7 Culturitalo
   Sturenkato 4
8 Enso-Gutzeit head office
   Kanavaranta 1
9 Academic Bookshop
   P. Esplanadikatu 39
10 Finlandia Concert Hall and Congress Wing
   Mannerheimintie 13
11 Otaniemi Technical University
   Main Building
   District heating and power plant
   University Library
   Students' Hostel

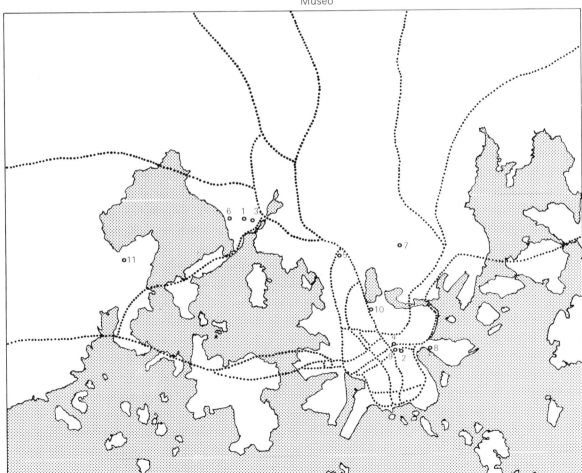

Civil Guard Building, Seinäjoki, 1925 ; street façade

Villa Väinölä, Alajärvi, c. 1926

Turun Sanomat, Turku, 1928–30

Apartment building, Turku, 1929

1930   Stadium and Sports Centre, Helsinki : competition entry

1930-31 University Hospital, Zagreb, Yugoslavia : competition entry

1931   University expansion, Helsinki : competition entry

1931   Cellulose factory, Toppila, near Oulu

1931   Lallukka, artists' housing, Helsinki : competition entry

1932   Prototype prefabricated house for the Insulite Co. : competition entry

1932   Weekend house for Enso-Gutzeit Co. : competition entry

1932-33 Sports stadium, Helsinki : competition entry

1933   Tuberculosis Sanatorium, Paimio

1933   Chairs for Paimio

1933   Housing for employees of the Sanatorium, Paimio

1933   Doctors' housing, Paimio

1933   Redevelopment plan for Norrmalm, Sweden : competition entry

1934   Railway station, Tampere : competition entry

1934   'Corso' restaurant interior, Zurich, Switzerland (with Max Ernst)

1934   Stenius housing development, Munkkiniemi : project

1934   National Exhibition Hall, Helsinki : competition entry, 3rd prize

1934   Central Post Office, Helsinki : competition entry

1935   Finnish Embassy, Moscow : competition entry

1935   Grave for Ahto Virtanen, Helsinki

1935   Municipal Library, Viipuri, now in the USSR (1927 competition entry won 1st prize)

1936 (?) Summer theatre, Alppila

1936   Plant and offices for ALKO (State Alcohol Monopoly) Helsinki : competition entry

1936   Finnish Pavilion at Paris World's Fair 1937 : competition entry, 1st prize

1936   Architect's own house, Munkkiniemi

1936   Art Museum, Tallinn (Reval), Estonia : competition entry

1937   Finnish Pavilion at Paris World's Fair

1937   Savoy restaurant interior, Helsinki

1937   'Savoy' vase

1937   Nordic United Bank, Karhula

1937-38 Extension to the University Library, Helsinki : competition entries (two phases), 2nd prize

1938   Two-storey row housing for Sunila

1938   Villa Mairea, Noormarkku

1938   Forestry Pavilion for the Agricultural Exhibition, Lapua

1938   Anjala Paper Factory, Inkeroinen

1938   Bloomberg Film Studio, Helsinki : project

1938-39 Terraced housing, Kauttua

1938-41 'A. Ahlström System', series of 'growing' summer cottages and detached houses

Employees' housing, Paimio, 1933: contemporary view showing balconies blocked in

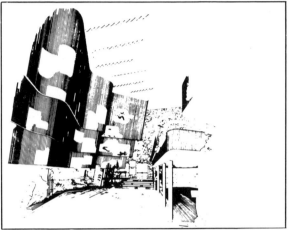

Finnish Pavilion, New York World Fair, 1938–39

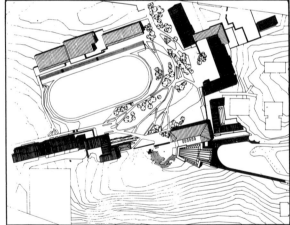

University, Jyväskylä, 1953: site plan

University, Jyväskylä: gymnasium and swimming pool

Housing for employees of the National Pensions Institute, Helsinki, 1954

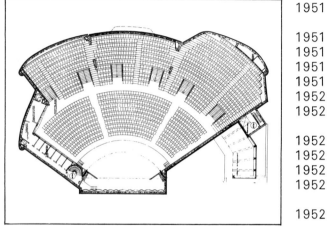

House of Culture, Helsinki, 1958 : auditorium plan

Church, Seinäjoki, 1960

Civic and Cultural Centre, Seinäjoki, 1960

1949	Villa Kihlman, Näsijärvi
1949	Ahlström factory warehouse, Karhula
1949	Sea harbour facilities, Helsinki : competition entry
1949	Town plan of Otaniemi : competition entry, 1st prize
1950	Tampella housing, Tampella
1950	Church, Lahti : competition entry, 1st prize
1950	Malm Funeral Chapel, Helsinki : competition entry, 1st prize
1950	Kivelä Hospital, Helsinki : competition entry
1950	University, Jyväskylä : project
1951	Erottaja Pavilion, Helsinki
1951	Regional Theatre, Kuopio : competition, 1st prize
1951	Funeral Chapel and Cemetery, Lyngby, Denmark : competition entry
1951	Enso-Gutzeit Paper Factory, Kotka
1951	Single-family house, Oulu
1951	Workers' housing, Inkeroinen
1951	M. S. Finntrader, boat interior
1952	Typpi Co. Sulphate Factory, Oulu
1952	Apartment building for the employees of Typpi Co., Oulu
1952	Town Hall, Säynätsalo
1952	Villa Manner, Sundby : project
1952	Sports hall, Otaniemi
1952	Building for the Association of Finnish Engineers, Helsinki
1952	Enso-Gutzeit Country Club, Kallvik, Helsinki
1952	National Pensions Building, Helsinki completed
1953	Architect's summer house, Muuratsalo
1953	Regional Plan for Imatra
1953	Enso-Gutzeit Paper Factory, Summa
1953—	University, Jyväskylä
1953	Sports hall and concert hall 'Vogelweidplatz', Vienna, Austria : competition entry
1954	Paper factory, Chandraghona, E. Pakistan
1954	Cellulose factory, housing, Sunila, Kotka
1954	Employees Housing, National Pensions Institute, Helsinki
1954	Studio R. S., Milan : project
1954	General plan for Kaskinen
1954	AERO housing, Helsinki : project
1954	Single-family housing, Pitäjänmäki, Helsinki
1954	Sports hall, Otaniemi, Espoo
1955	Bank, Baghdad, Iraq : project
1955	Theatre and concert hall, Oulu : project
1955	Soldiers' Memorial, Alajärvi
1955	Regional plan for Lappland
1955	Rautatalo office building, Helsinki
1956	Architect's studio, Munkkiniemi, Helsinki
1956	Main Railway Station, Göteborg, Sweden : project
1956	Master plan, University, Oulu
1956	Cemetery extension, Alarjärvi

1956	Finnish Pavilion, Venice Biennale
1956	Director's (of Typpi Co.) house, Oulu
1956	Sets for Metropolitan Opera House, New York
1957	Apartment building, Hansaviertel, West Berlin, Germany
1957	Town Hall, Göteberg, Sweden : competition entry, 1st prize
1957	Town Hall, Marl, West Germany : competition project
1958	House of Culture, Helsinki
1958	Kampenentsbacken Housing Development Project, Stockholm, Sweden : competition entry, 1st prize
1958 (?)	Town Hall Hufvusta, Stockholm, Sweden : project
1958	Town Hall, Kiruna, Sweden : competition entry, 1st prize
1958	National Bank of Iraq, Baghdad, Iraq : project
1958	Art Museum, Baghdad, Iraq : project
1958	Church at Vuoksenniska, Imatra
1958	Building for Postal Administration, Baghdad, Iraq : project
1959	Villa Carré, Bazoches-sur-Guyonne, France
1959	Opera House, Essen, Germany, first project : competition entry, 1st prize
1959	Karhusaari housing development, Espoo : project
1960	Church, Seinäjoki
1960	Civic and Cultural Centre, Seinäjoki
1960	Finnish War Memorial, Suomussalmi
1960	Aalto family tomb, Alajärvi
1961	Sundh Centre, Avesta, Sweden
1961	Korkalovaara housing, Rovaniemi
1961	Shopping centre, Otaniemi, Espoo
1961	Power station, Lieksankoski, Lieksa
1961	Power station, Pankakoski
1961	High-rise apartments, Viitaniemi Jyväskylä
1961	Project for the city centre, Helsinki
1961-76	Opera House Essen, W. Germany : competition entry 1958
1962	Neue Vahr, high-rise apartment building, Bremen, W. Germany
1962	Folk Museum of Central Finland, Jyväskylä
1962	Parish centre, Wolfsburg, W. Germany
1962	Residential and commercial building, Rovaniemi
1962	Cultural Centre, Leverkusen, W. Germany : project
1962	Enso-Gutzeit building, Helsinki
1962	Enskilda Banken building, Stockholm, Sweden : competition entry, 2nd prize
1962	Stockmann department store, Helsinki : project
1963	Cultural Centre, Wolfsburg, W. Germany
1963	Thermo-technical laboratories, Institute of Technology, Otaniemi
1963	Housing, Rovaniemi : project
1963	Boiler house, Institute of Technology, Otaniemi, Espoo
1963	Town plan for Otaniemi, Espoo

Korkalovaara Housing, Rovaniemi, 1961

Shopping centre, Otaniemi, 1961

Residential and commercial building with sculpture by Aalto, Rovaniemi, 1962

Town Hall, Seinäjoki, 1965

Interior of Main Auditorium, Institute of Technology,
Otaniemi, 1964. Photo Ingervo

Family house, Rovaniemi, 1965

Interior of swimming pool, University, Jyväskylä, 1966

Library, Institute of Technology, Otaniemi, 1969

1963	Parish centre, Detmerode, W. Germany : project
1964	Interiors of the Institute of International Education, New York, USA
1964	Project for the city centre, Helsinki
1964	Main building, Institute of Technology, Otaniemi, Espoo
1964	Office building for Pohjoismaiden Yhdyspankki, Helsinki
1964	BP administrative building, Hamburg, W. Germany : competition entry, 3rd prize
1964	Wood Technology Laboratories, Otaniemi, Espoo
1964	Administrative building for the City Electrical Co., Helsinki : project
1964	Extensions to Paimio Sanatorium
1965	Town Hall, Seinäjoki
1965	Municipal Library, Seinäjoki
1965	Vastmanland-Dala Student Union, Uppsala, Sweden
1965	Heilig-Geist-Gemeinde Kindergarten, Wolfsburg, W. Germany : project
1965	Administrative and Cultural Centre, Jyväskylä : project
1965	Administrative building for the Pohjola Insurance Co., Helsinki : competition entry
1965	Single-family house, Rovaniemi
1965	Town centre, Castrop-Rauxel, W. Germany : competition entry
1965	Extensions to the University, Jyväskylä
1966	Student hostel, Otaniemi
1966	Terraced housing, Pietarsaari
1966	Swimming pool, University, Jyväskylä
1966	Student Union, University, Jyväskylä
1966	Parish hall, Seinäjoki
1966	Urban design project for Stensvik
1966	Experimental town project for Gammelbacka, Porvoo
1966	Mixed development at San Lanfranco, Pavia, Italy : project
1966	Cultural Centre, Siena, Italy : project
1966	Theatre, Wolfsburg, W. Germany : project
1966-78	Parish centre, Riola, Bologna, Italy
1966	Prototype for the administration building and warehouse of the Societá Ferrero, Turin, Italy
1966	Terraced housing, Jacobstad
1967	Art Museum Lehtinen, Kuusisaari, Helsinki : project
1967	Town plan, Rovaniemi : project
1967	Ekenäs Savings Bank, Tammisaari
1967	Parish centre, Zurich-Altstetten, Switzerland : project
1968	Parish centre, Detmerode, W. Germany
1968	Schonbuhl high-rise apartment building, Lucerne, Switzerland
1968	Scandinavian House, Reykjavik, Iceland
1968	Library, Rovaniemi
1969	Library, Institute of Technology, Otaniemi
1969	Shopping centre, Tammisaari

1969	Town Hall, Alajärvi
1969	Library, Kokkola : project
1969	Academic Bookshop, Helsinki
1969	Kokkonen House, Järvenpää
1969	Water tower, Institute of Technology, Otaniemi
1969	Sauna and summer house, Päjänne
1969	Municipal Theatre, Seinäjoki : project
1970	Sports Institute, University, Jyväskylä
1970	Mount Angel Benedictine College Library, Salem, Oregon, USA
1970	Parish centre, Alajärvi
1970	Villa Schildt, Tammisaari
1970	Police Headquarters, Jyväskylä (part of the Administrative and Cultural Centre)
1970 (?)	Theatre, Alajärvi : project
1970	Museum of Modern Art, Shiraz, Iran : project
1971	Finlandia Concert Hall, Helsinki
1971	Extensions to the Institute of Technology, Otaniemi
1972	Project for the city centre, Helsinki
1972	Villa Erica, Turin, Italy : project
1973	Art Museum, Aalborg, Denmark (with Elissa Aalto and Jean-Jacques Barvel)
1973	Alvar Aalto Museum, Jyväskylä
1973	Fire-testing laboratory, Otaniemi
1974	Administrative building for the City Electric Co., Helsinki
1974	Enso-Gutzeit administrative building annexe, Helsinki : project
1974	Sculpture for the Finnish Embassy, Brasilia, Brazil
1975	Lappia House, Theatre and Congress Hall, Rovaniemi
1975	Congress Wing of the Finlandia Hall, Helsinki
1975	Mid-West Institute of Scandinavian Culture, Eau Claire, Wisconsin, USA
1976	University of Reykjavik, Iceland : project
1978	Church, Lahti
1978	City office building, Jyväskylä (part of the Administrative and Cultural Centre)
1976	Died 11th May

Town Hall, Alajärvi, 1969

Police headquarters, Jyväskylä, 1970

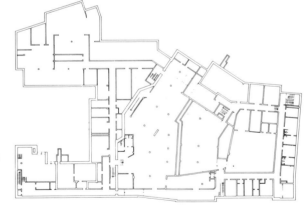

Lappia House, Rovaniemi, 1975 : basement plan

Bibliography

Selected Writings by Aalto (arranged chronologically)

'Postwar Reconstruction: Rehousing Research in Finland', published privately in New York, 1940.
'The Humanising of Architecture', *Architectural Forum*, Vol. 73, December 1940.
'Designing Today's Furniture', *Interiors*, Vol. 100, June 1941.
'The RIBA Annual Discourse', *RIBA Journal*, Vol. 64, May 1957.
'Sigfried Giedion in Memoriam 10.4.68', *Arkitekten*, Vol. 65 No. 2, 1968.

Selected Books

G. Baird and Y. Futogawa, *Alvar Aalto*, London, 1970.
P. Beal, 'Non-Scandinavian Bibliography of Alvar Aalto', *American Association of Architectural Bibliographers Papers*, Vol. 5, 1968, pp. 95-106.
C. Cresti, *Alvar Aalto*, Florence, 1975.
K. Fleig (ed.), *Alvar Aalto I, 1922-62*, Zürich, 1963.
K. Fleig (ed.), *Alvar Aalto II, 1963-70*, Zürich, 1971.
K. Fleig (ed.), *Alvar Aalto*, Zürich, 1974. English version, New York, 1975.
Y. Futogawa, 'La Maison Louis Carré', *Global Architecture No. 10*, Tokyo.
Y. Futogawa, 'Church in Vuoksenniska (Imatra); City Centre in Seinäjoki', *Global Architecture No. 16*, Tokyo.
Y. Futogawa, 'Town Hall at Säynätsalo; National Pensions Building in Helsinki', *Global Architecture No. 24*, Tokyo.
F. Gutheim, *Alvar Aalto*, London, 1960.
W. C. Miller, *CPL Exchange Bibliography 1190: Alvar Aalto*, Council of Planning Librarians, POB 229, Monticello, Illinois 61856, USA.
E. and C. Neuenschwander, *Alvar Aalto and Finnish Architecture*, London, 1954.
P. D. Pearson, *Alvar Aalto and the International Style*, John Whitney & Sons, New York, 1978. (Based on a PhD thesis of the same title, University of London, 1977.)
G. Schildt, *Luonnoksia*, Otava, Helsinki, 1972.

Selected Articles

'Happy Birthday Baker House, Aalto's MIT Dormitory is 25 years old', S. Abercrombie, *Architecture Plus*, Vol. 1, July 1973.
'Criticism of the North Jutland Museum of Arts, Aalborg, Denmark', M. Brawne, *Architectural Review*, Vol. 153, March 1973.
'Paimio Sanatorium: an analysis', W. R. Bunning, *Architecture* (Sydney), Vol. 29, February 1940.
'Finland and architect Aalto', J. E. Burchard, *Architectural Record*, Vol. 125, January 1959.

'Benedictins pas morts—III: la Bibliothèque de Mount Angel (Oregon)', Dom. F. Debuyst, *Art d'Eglise*, Vol. 39, No. 154, 1971.
'Les maîtres de l'Architecture Nouvelle en Finlande, pays des mille lacs: Alvar Aalto', P. L. Flouquet, *Bâtir*, October 1938.
'Aalto in Italia', F. Fogh, *Arkitektur* (Denmark), Vol. 16, No. 1, 1972.
'Alvar Aalto', S. Giedion, *Architectural Review*, Vol. 107, February 1950.
'Alvar Aalto', H. H. Goldstone, *Magazine of Art*, Vol. 32, April 1939.
'Alvar Aalto Today', F. Gutheim, *Architectural Record*, Vol. 133, April 1963.
'Aalto vs. Aalto: the other Finland', H.-R. Hitchcock, *Perspecta* Nos. 9/10, 1965.
'Alvar Aalto', *Cuadernos de Arcquitectura*, No. 72, 1967, J. Llorens, with the text of a letter from Vico Magistretti discussing Aalto.
'Presentation of the Royal Gold Medal for 1957 to Professor Alvar Aalto', Sir Leslie Martin, *RIBA Journal*, Vol. 64, May 1957.
'A Man Standing in the Center', W. McQuade, *Architectural Forum*, Vol. 125, No. 1, January/February 1967.
'Viipuri Library, Finland', P. Morton Shand, *Architectural Review*, Vol. 79, March 1936.
'Il Nuovo Studio di Alvar Aalto a Munkkiniemi', L. Mosso, *Casabella Continuità*, No. 217, 1957.
'La Maison Carré, L. Mosso, *Casabella Continuità*, No. 236, February 1960.
'Nel Centro Storico di Helsinki la Sede Enso-Gutzeit di Alvar Aalto', L. Mosso, *Casabella Continuità*, No. 272, February 1963.
'La luce nell'architettura di Alvar Aalto', L. Mosso, *Zodiac*, No. 7, 1960.
'Alvar Aalto at Mount Angel Abbey', B. Reasoner, *Journal of the Society of Architectural Historians*, Vol. 31, No. 3, October 1972.
'Aalto up to date', W. Segal, *Architects' Journal*, Vol. 155, No. 17, 26th April 1972.
'Aalto revisited', B. P. Spring, *Architectural Forum*, Vol. 124, No. 3, April 1966.
'Une Maison d'Aalto en Ile de France', G. Veronese, *Zodiac*, No. 6, 1960.

Memorial Issues of Magazines

Arkkitehti, July/August 1976.
L'Architecture d'Aujourd'hui, June 1977.
Space Design, January/February 1977.

Exhibition Catalogues

'Aalto: architecture and furniture', The Museum of Modern Art, New York, 1938.
'Alvar Aalto', Giorgia Labò, Milan, 1948.
'L'opera di Alvar Aalto', catalogue of exhibition arranged by L. Mosso, Milan, 1965.
'Alvar Aalto 1898-1976', Memorial Exhibition, The Museum of Finnish Architecture, Helsinki, 1978.

Alvar Aalto: Résumé

Aalto demeure le plus énigmatique des maîtres du Mouvement Moderne. Des dessins, des photographies et des peintures de Aalto ont été publiés en trois épais volumes ; nous savons cependant qu'il ne s'agit là en aucune façon de l'oeuvre complète. Le fait d'être un grand individualiste et ne même temps l'un des deux plus grands architectes scandinaves de ce siècle, avec Gunnar Asplund, l'entoure en quelque sorte d'une aura. Et peut-être cette aura a-t-elle prévenu une appréhension de la totalité de son oeuvre, bien que ses maisons individuelles aient fait l'objet d'une critique raisonnée et pénétrante.

Le moment est venu d'ouvrir le débat sur l'oeuvre de Aalto au niveau que Venturi suggérait dans *Complexité et Contradiction en Architecture;* c'est-à-dire d'affronter les paradoxes de son oeuvre qui, depuis 1927, a été résolument moderne tout en dédaignant les lois de cohérence et d'expression inhérentes au Mouvement Moderne. Work a déjà commencé à répertorier la remarquable transition opérée par Aalto entre son vernaculaire néo-classique et son plein épanouissement comme Moderniste. Cette voie fut également suivie par Le Corbusier et Mies van der Rohe, et pour ce dernier, *Architectural Monograph* prévoit un numéro qui traitera de cette transition extensivement.

Ce numéro d'*Architectural Monograph* est plus descriptif que d'habitude et il comprend trois analyses pertinentes des aspects de l'oeuvre de Aalto. D'autres réalisations doivent être produites par le bureau qui continue son activité sous la direction de la veuve de Aalto, Madame Elissa Aalto. La production de ce bureau depuis les années vingt s'élève à plus de 300 constructions et projets, et certains indices permettent de s'attendre à ce que d'autres soient découverts. Les limites de la publication ont fait que seule une petite partie de cette oeuvre importante a pu être considérée. La première section s'intéresse aux constructions de la période de transition entre le vernaculaire néoclassique et le Modernisme. La seconde est une exploration d'un genre de constructions, dans ce cas les Bibliothèques. Puis l'étude de la petite maison d'été de Aalto et de son bureau/atelier s'oppose à celle d'un de ses plans de grand ensemble, et nous finissons par une série de constructions révélatrices de son talent et de son génie ; cette sélection se termine par une chronologie aussi complète que possible.

Dans le passage où il explique ces essais, Porphyrios écrit : 'Je propose de retrouver (la sensibilité qui ordonne et gouverne l'oeuvre de Aalto) dans les zones constitutives de la production architecturale suivantes : 1. la syntaxe planimétrique et sectionnelle (l'organisation du plan et de la section) ; 2. la *taxinomie* de la fonction (la classification du programme) ; la *taxinomie* de la représentation sensuelle (l'organisation des thèmes iconographiques).'

La première catégorie de la syntaxe planimétrique et sectionnelle est analysée après que soit établie l'opposition dialectique avec l'*homotopie*, 'royaume du même', en ces termes : 'Il existe une sensibilité qui distribue la multiplicité des objets existants en catégories que le regard orthodoxe du Modernisme serait incapable de nommer, de décrire ou de penser ; je veux dire ce sens particulier de l'ordre dans lequel des fragments d'un certain nombre de cohérences possibles miroitent séparément sans qu'une loi commune les unifie. Cet ordre, dont le rationnalisme occidental se défie et qu'il a arbitrairement classé comme désordre, nous l'appellerons *hétéropie* ; ce mot doit être pris dans son sens le plus littéral, comme désignant l'état d'objets posés, placés, situés à des emplacements si différents l'un de l'autre qu'il est impossible de définir un lieu commun entre eux tous.'

Comme exemple, Porphyrios donne 'le Centre Culturel de Wolfsburg (où) un certain nombre de cohérences géométriques semblent s'être constituées par hasard : la grille en étoile des salles de conférences, la disposition introvertie de la bibliothèque et la grille en forme d'orthogone irrégulier des bureaux, des installations communes et des espaces auxiliaires. Là les discontinuités sont bienvenues. L'exigence homotopique d'une ordre continu est abandonnée et des hiatus importants sont introduits. La syntaxe ne comporte pas de gradations, ne comporte aucune nuance. Au contraire, des espaces vides et des discontinuités soudaines entourent les limites de chaque zone, brisant la construction en fragments syntaxiques, puis juxtaposant ces fragments, ne donnant aucun indice qui puisse aider à la reconstitution du puzzle perdu, ne laissant que des traces difficiles à déchiffrer . . .'

Utilisant les catégories rhétoriques de la *discriminatio* et de la *convenientia*, Porphyrios remarque que cette approche caractérise Richardson en Amérique, le *Volk-Kultur-Primitiv* en Allemagne, la *Free School* en Angleterre et bien d'autres parmi lesquels il souligne notamment les exemples scandinaves de J. H. Palme, J. F. Willumsen et Aksel Gallen-Kallela.

La *taxinomie* de la fonction chez Aalto n'est expressive ni de la fonction ni de la structure ; 'bien que séparés par un intervalle de vingt huit ans, l'Institut de Technologie d'Otaniemi et le Sanatorium de Paimio partagent la même aspiration à une composition volumétrique hétéro-topique. Il serait vain de vouloir réduire tout le champ du visible à un système de variables puis de vouloir établir entre elles les relations d'une classification fonctionnelle. Au contraire, la composition se présente sans continuité essentielle ; un champ visuel qui est énoncé dès l'origine dans la forme de la fragmentation, de la discontinuité, de l'incohérence, de la divergence ou de la discordance.'

La *taxinomie* de la représentation sensuelle qui s'enrichit d'une comparaison entre Jyväskyla et la Villa Savoie à Poissy est ensuite analysée en relation avec la célèbre cour de la maison de Aalto à Muuratsalo 'où se déploie et s'affronte sans retenue la grande variété de briques et de tuiles d'une façon qui évoque la profusion exubérante d'une couverture en *patchwork*. On trouve là par excellence la conscience du dossier, où les objets sont transformés pour être sauvés de la disparition : ici, le champ visuel signale partout son spectacle, découvrant ses similarités, ses différences, ses légendes associatives ou sa matérialité sensuelle chargée d'histoire.'

Porphyrios conclut que 'l'*hétérotopie* a joué un rôle critique quoique silencieux vis-à-vis des priorités de la société occidentale. Au niveau de la syntaxe planimétrique et sectionnelle elle a été la négation des codifications de construction que nécessitait la production industrialisée, opposant la ligne d'assemblage à la standardisation absolue de l'industrie du bâtiment et à la préséance de la *tekhnê* (technique du travail). Au niveau de la *taxinomie* de la fonction, elle s'est opposée à l'interprétation de l'architecture comme science et non comme art, évitant par là-mème la stérilité quantitative du Fonctionnalisme aussi bien que ses conséquences secondaires et tertiaires qui ont affligé les attitudes de la pensée architecturale des années cinquante et soixante, comme l'analyse des données socioéconomiques, les enquêtes auprès des utilisateurs et coetera. Au niveau de la *taxinomie* de la représentation sensuelle, l'*hétérotopie* a combattu l'image d'entreprise et l'universalité du style International, non pas pour défendre le régionalisme et le nationalisme, mais pour souligner le caractère non-consommable de l'objet architectural.' Malgré ses positions en recul, 'la signification de la sensibilité hétérotopique (de Aalto) réside essentiellement dans le fait qu'elle a fait écran au positivisme, ainsi qu'aux alliances que ce positivisme entretenait implicitement avec la production industrialisée et le gaspillage de la société de consommation' . . .

Raija-Liisa Heinonen décrit dans son essai la toile de fond des premières années d'apprentissage de Aalto. 'Les pays scandinaves entretenaient d'étroites relations, non seulement sur le plan géographique, mais aussi sur le plan linguistique. La langue des gens cultivés en Finlande était le suédois ... le seul magazine d'architecture en Finlande, *Arkkitehti-Arkitekton*, était publié en deux éditions séparées, l'une en finlandais, l'autre en suédois ... Il n'y eut pas cependant que la Suède qui prit de l'importance dans les années vingt. L'influence de l'Italie se faisait sentir encore davantage. Le programme de l'Université de Technologie insistait sur le Baroque et la Renaissance Italienne, et il était évident que, pour les jeunes architectes qui voyageaient après la guerre, l'Italie était par excellence la terre d'inspiration.' Ce n'était pas seulement les constructions monumentales qui retenaient leur attention, mais les formes cubistes du vernaculaire mediterranéen.

'Bien que l'idée d'établir une relation entre l'intérieur et la nature vienne de l'architecture italienne, Aalto avait nettement à l'esprit les conditions finlandaises, où l'on passe beaucoup de temps à l'intérieur durant la mauvaise saison. Selon lui, 'une maison finlandaise devrait avoir deux visages. L'un de ces visages est le contact esthétique direct avec l'extérieur ; l'autre, le visage de l'hiver, apparait dans les formes de la décoration intérieure qui correspond à nos sentiments les plus intimes.' Par la suite, ce motif de l'atrium, qui se développe dans certains cas en piazza, apparut fréquemment, bien que soumis à de grandes variations.'

Comment cette sensibilité se situait-elle dans le développement international ? 'En avril 1928, la conférence annuelle de la SAFA eut lieu à Turku. Sven Markelius, de Stockholm, fut invité à faire un exposé, sans doute à la demande de Aalto et de Bryggman ... Hildung Ekelund affirma par la suite que cet exposé avait marqué l'avènement du Fonctionnalisme en Finlande.' Cet été-là, 'Aino et Alvar Aalto voyagèrent en France, en Hollande et au Danemark pour voir la nouvelle architecture. Bryggman et Ilmari Ahonen voyagèrent en Allemagne, s'arrêtant à Stuttgart pour visiter le Weissenhofsiedlung, à Francfort où ils virent les projets d'habitations de Ernst May et à Dessau où ils rencontrèrent Gropius.'

Madame Heinonen décrit ensuite les interventions de Aalto dans divers concours, soit qu'il y présentât projets, soit qu'il fît partie du jury. Elle conclut que la contribution d'Alvar Aalto est de la plus grande importance dans l'introduction du Fonctionnalisme en Finlande. Il fut le premier architecte finlandais à entrer en contact avec la nouvelle idéologie et la nouvelle architecture, à les faire connaître et à les réaliser dans ses propres constructions. Il semble également avoir assimilé les contenus idéologiques du Fonctionnalisme sans s'égarer à suivre dogmatiquement son programme.

L'essai de Steven Groák s'attache à l'analyse de trois aspects interdépendants des constructions de Aalto. 'Tout d'abord ... il y a le rôle dominant de la lumière dans l'oeuvre de Aalto, que certains considèrent comme ayant une fonction d'harmonisation. En second lieu, il y a le traitement de la clôture de l'espace, et la conception, qui en découle, de l'espace réalisé dans ses constructions, qui permet l'analyse d'un certain nombre d'éléments du plan – le thème de l'atrium central, la voie fonctionnelle, la nature des murs intérieurs et extérieurs. Enfin, il y a l'utilisation extensive de la décoration sur toutes les surfaces et, en particulier, son rôle pour créer différentes 'strates' dans ces surfaces.

Cela doit aboutir à un 'effet de dématérialisation' du mur chez Aalto, et Groák ajoute que 'les édifices (peuvent) être considérés comme des objets se trouvant à l'intersection de deux chemins – celui suivi par le soleil autour de l'édifice et celui emprunté par l'observateur qui tourne autour ou y pénètre. (Et à l'occasion, la forme du bâti est conçue métaphoriquement comme un 'éventail', avec ce que cela suppose sur la signification originelle de cette forme). En ce sens, tous les murs et surfaces servent simultanément à contrôler, dévier ou redistribuer la lumière qui pénètre l'édifice ou s'y réfléchit, et à marquer les différents itinéraires. Il ne s'agit pas d'une coincidence, mais presque d'une conséquence nécessaire de cette proposition, si beaucoup des édifices ont plusieurs entrées. Cependant, on peut observer dans bien des cas – et plus particulièrement pour les constructions publiques de grande ou moyenne taille – qu'un changement fonctionnel dans l'itinéraire est marqué par un changement de niveau et qu'il est dès lors très important de voir où et comment les escaliers sont placés.' Il apparaît donc que l'oeuvre de Aalto peut être considérée comme possédant une logique qui ordonne l'exploitation du site comme le plus petit détail.

Pour faire une démonstration de cette idée, Groák analyse l'utilisation de la décoration chez Aalto. 'A partir des années trente, Aalto semble s'être de plus en plus intéressé aux possibilités décoratives des matériaux 'en eux-même'. Le mur expérimental de Muuratsalo est bien connu. La centrale électrique d'Otaniemi peut presque être interprétée parfois comme un essai pour représenter les possibilités du matériau opaque en opposition au verre du Sanatorium de Paimio. Son utilisation du marbre blanc présente un intérêt certain. Il est essentiellement utilisé à Otaniemi comme repère – il marque l'entrée de la Bibliothèque et, de l'autre côté du parc, il est utilisé pour la façade de l'Ecole d'Architecture, dans un style qui semble une plaisanterie délibérée dans sa référence au passé. L'exploitation du marbre pour les surfaces de la Salle de Concert Finlandia semble une complète réussite. Le marbre est utilisé à la fois comme écran, devant et derrière des escaliers, et comme surface réfléchissante. Il permet de se rendre compte qu'Aalto, dans sa conception de l'édifice, prévoyait que celui-ci serait vu à différentes heures du jour et à différents moments de l'année.

Groák conclut que à ses yeux 'les constructions d'Aalto ... existent en tant qu'objets qui combinent les systèmes de voies d'activité pour les gens et le système des sources possibles de lumière. L'utilisation de la décoration est dès lors une partie dans un ensemble complexe de moyens par lesquels les éléments muraux en particulier sont 'dématérialisés' pour signifier cette pénétration et cette combinaison. Par delà cette approche ... l'utilisation de l'espace chez Aalto semble assez libre à la limite, mais la définition et la clôture du bâti ne sont jamais réellement transparentes. Aalto demeure étrange, mais peut-être sans être mystérieux ; il semble toujours préoccupé de donner à l'utilisateur des clefs pour comprendre la nature de son architecture'.

Alvar Aalto: Resümee

Aalto ist bis heute der rätselhafteste unter den Meistern des Modern Movement geblieben. Drei dicke Bände voll von Zeichnungen, Fotos und Aaltos Bildern sind herausgekommen, und doch wissen wir, dass sie in keiner Weise das komplette *oeuvre* darstellen.

Irgendwie ist er von der Aura umgeben, ein grosser Individualist zu sein, und gleichzeitig einer der beiden grössten skandinavischen Architekten dieses Jahrhunderts, wobei der andere Gunnar Asplund ist. Und vielleicht hat diese Aura die Diskussion über die Gesammtheit seines Werks verhindert, obwohl einzelne Bauten eindringlicher Kritik und tiefgehender Betrachtungen gewürdigt worden sind.

Es ist nun an der Zeit, die Diskussion über Aalto zu eröffnen auf der Ebene, die Venturi in seinem Buch *Vielschichtigkeit und Widerspruch in der Architektur* vorgeschlagen hat. Das heisst, fertigzuwerden mit den Gegensätzen in seinem Werk, das seit 1927 entschieden modern gewesen ist, jedoch nie den Spielregeln des Modern Movement gehorcht hat, was Konsequenz und Ausdruck anbelangt. Man hat inzwischen angefangen, Aaltos bemerkenswerten Ubergang von der klassizistischen Formensprache zu den vollerblühten Ausdrucksformen der Moderne zu katalogisieren. Auch Le Corbusier und Mies van der Rohe sind diesem Weg gefolgt. Der Ubergang von Letzterem soll demnächst in einer *Architectural Monographs* ausführlich behandelt werden.

Dies ist eine *Architectural Monographs* mehr im eigentlichen Sinn des Wortes als gewöhnlich, indem sie drei wichtige Diskussionen über Aspekte von Aaltos Werk beinhaltet. Weitere Bauten sind von seinem Büro versprochen worden, das von seiner Witwe, Frau Elissa Aalto weitergeführt wird. Der Ausstoss dieses Büros beläuft sich seit den 20iger Jahren auf mehr als 300 Gebäude und Projekte, und es gibt Hinweise, dass bald noch mehr entdeckt werden könnten. Aus reinen Platzgründen konnte nur eine kleine Auswahl von diesem umfangreichen Werk getroffen worden. Die erste Gruppe umfasst Gebäude aus der Ubergangsperiode vom Klassizismus zur Moderne. Zweitens die Erforschung eines bestimmten Gebäudetyps, in diesem Fall Bibliotheken. Dann wurde sein eigenes kleines Sommerhaus und Studio seinen Wohnungsbauten gegenübergestellt. Und Schliesslich wählten wir eine Reihe von Gebäuden, die seine Genialität und sein Können zeigen. Diese Auswahl ist abgerundet durch eine Chronologie, die so genau ist wie derzeit möglich.

Zusammengefasst ausgedrückt sagt Porphyrios: 'Ich schlage vor, (die ordnende Sensibilität, die Aaltos Werk beherrscht), in den folgenden wesentlichen Gebieten der Architekturproduktion aufzuspüren, insbesondere erstens in der Syntax von Grundrissen und Schnitten, zweitens der Taxinomie der Funktion (der Klassifizierung des Programms) und drittens der Taxinomie der sinnlichen Darstellung (die Organisation der ikonografishcen Themen).'

Die erste Kategorie der Syntax von Grundrissen und Schnitten wird diskutiert, nachdem der dialektische Gegensatz von homotopie – das Reich der Gleichheit – mit den folgenden Worten formuliert wird: 'Es gibt eine Sensibilität, die die Vielfältigkeit der vorhandenen Dinge in Kategorien einteilt, die der orthodoxe flüchtige Blick der Moderne kaum imstande wäre zu benennen, oder in ihnen zu denken oder zu reden. Ich meine diesen seltsamen Sinn für Ordnung, wo Fragmente einer Auswahl von möglichen Zusammenhängen separat glitzern ohne eine vereinende, gemeinsame Gesetzmässigkeit. Diese Art von Ordnung, die vom westlichen Rationalismus mit Misstrauen betrachtet wird, und abwertend Unordnung genannt wird, wollen wir heterotopia nennen. Dieses Wort sollte so wörtlich wie möglich genommen werden, das heisst, die waltenden Umstände wiesen so unterschiedliche Bauplätze an, dass es unmöglich ist, einen ihnen allen gemeinsamen locus zu definieren.'

Als Beispiel zitiert Porphyrios das Wolfsburger Kulturzentrum, wo eine Anzahl von geometrischen Zusammenhängen scheinbar durch den reinsten Zufall zusammengebracht worden sind. Das strahlenförmige Raster der Hörsäale, die introvertierte Anordnung der Bibliothek und das ungleichmässige Raster der Büros, der Gemeinschaftsräume und der Nebenräume. Hier sind Unterbrechungen willkommen. Die homotope Notwendigkeit einer fortlaufenden Ordnung ist über Bord geworfen, an deren Stelle grosse Sprünge eingeführt werden. Die Formensprache wird nicht abgestuft, nie werden unmerkliche Ubergänge geschaffen. Statt dessen umschreiben Leerräume und plötzliche Lücken die Grenzen eines jeden Bereichs und zerteilen das Gebäude in syntaktische Fragmente, um diese dann untereinander sich gegenüberzustellen und geben keinen Hinweis, der das verlorengegangene Puzzle erklären würde und hinterlassen nichts als Spuren, die schwer zu entziffern sind.

Indem Porphyrios die rhetorischen Kategorien der discriminatio und der convenientia benutzt, weist er darauf hin, dass diese Art vorzugehen für Richardson in Amerika (das Volk-Kultur-Primitiv in Deutschland) die englische *free school* und viele andere charakteristisch ist und hebt die skandinavischen Beispiele von J. H. Palme, J. F. Willumsen und Aksel Gallen-Kallela hervor.

Die Taxinomie der Funktion drückt bei Aalto weder den Zweck noch das konstruktive Gefüge aus. Obwohl 28 Jahre auseinander, zeigt die Technische Hochschule von Otaniemi dieselbe Lust an heterotopischer räumlicher Komposition wie das Paimio Sanatorium. Es würde zu nichts führen, reduzierte man die ganze Skala des Sichtbaren auf ein System von Variablen und versuchte dann, sie mittels einer Einteilung nach Funktionen zu verbinden. Stattdessen präsentiert sich die Komposition selbst ohne wesentliche Kontinuität. Es handelt sich hier um eine Sichtbarkeit, die von Anfang an auf der Form der Fragmentierung, der Diskontinuität, der Inkonsequenz, der Abweichung und der Disharmonie beruht.

Die Taxinomie der Sinnlichen Darstellung, der der Vergleich zwischen Jyväskyla und der Villa Savoie in Poissy sehr zum Vorteil gereicht, wird dann im Zusammenhang mit dem berühmten Innenhof von Aaltos Sommerhaus in Muuratsalo diskutiert, wo die grosse Vielfalt von Ziegel – und Kachelwerk sich ganz ungehemmt entfaltet in der Art des wilden Uberflusses einer Patchworkdecke. Es handelt sich hier in unübertroffener Weise um die Vorstellung von einem Dossier, wo Dinge abgeheftet werden, um vor dem Untergang bewahrt zu werden: hier entfaltet die Sichtbarkeit ihr ganzes Spektakel, stellt ihre Ahnlichkeiten, ihre Unterschiede, die Legenden, die sich mit ihr verbinden, oder ihre historisch belastete Körperlichkeit dar.

Porphyrios kommt zu dem Schluss, dass 'heterotopie eine kritische, wenn auch stumme Rolle den Prioritäten der westlichen Welt genenüber spielte. Auf der Ebene der Syntax von Grundrissen und Schnitten verleugnet sie die Kodifizierung der Konstruktion, die die industrielle Produktion erfordert, und schützt auf diese Weise vor der absoluten Standardisierung der Bauindustrie und der Ablösung der techne (Arbeitstechnik) durch das Fliessband. Auf der Ebene der Taxinomie der Funktion hält sie der Interpretation von Architektur als Wissenschaft statt Kunst stand und vermeidet so sowohl die quantitativ bestimmbare Sterilität des Funktionalismus als auch seine sekundären und tertiären Konsequenzen, die architektonisches Denken in den 50iger und 60iger Jahren plagten wie sozioökonomische Datenanalyse und Verbrauchererbefregungen usw. Auf der Ebene der Taxinomie der sinnlichen Darstellung kämpfte heterotopia gegen das Image des Unternehmerischen und die allgemeine Verbreitung des Internationalen Stils, nicht etwa um Regionalismus oder Nationalismus zu verteidigen, sondern um die Nichtkonsumierbarkeit des architektonishen Objekts zu unterstreichen. Trotz aller Nachteile bestand die Bedeutung von Aaltos heterotopischer Sensibilität im wesentlichen darin, dass sie den Positivismus zugleich mit seiner Verbindung zu industrieller Produktion und Verbraucherverschwendung dämpfte.'

Raija-Liisa Heinonens Essay beschreibt den Hintergrund der Anfangszeit in Aaltos Schaffen: 'die skandinavischen Länder standen in engem Kontakt zueinander, nicht nur geographisch, sondern auch linguistisch. Die Sprache der Akademiker in Finnland war Schwedisch, die einzige Architekturzeitschrift *Arkkitehti-Arikitekton* kam in zwei getrennten Auflagen heraus, eine auf Finnisch, eine auf Schwedisch. Schweden war jedoch nicht das einzige wichtige Land in den 20iger Jahren. Der Einfluss von Italien wurde immer deutlicher. Der Lehrplan der Technischen Hochschule hatte seinen Schwerpunkt auf italienischer Rennaissance und Barock und es war klar, wenn Architekten nach dem Krieg reisten, dass Italien des Ziel ihrer Wünsche war. Es waren nicht nur die grossartigen Bauwerke, die ihre Aufmerksamkeit auf sich zogen, sondern auch die kubistischen Formen der Mittelmeerarchitektur.

'Obwohl die Idee, den Innenraum mit der Natur zu verbinden, von der italienischen Architektur stammt, hatte Aalto ganz klar die finnischen Gegebenheiten im Sinn, wo die meiste Zeit während der Wintermonate im Hause verbraucht wird. Seiner Meinung nach sollte ein finnisches Haus zwei Gesichter haben. Das eine besteht im direkten Kontakt mit der Aussenwelt, das andere, das Wintergesicht wird in der Form der Innenraumgestaltung sichtbar, die unsere verborgensten Gefühle wiederspiegelt. Später erscheint dieses Atriummotiv – in einigen Fällen als Piazza – oft, obwohl mit vielen Adwandelungen.'

In welchem Verhältnis stand dieses Gefühl zur internationalen Entwicklung? 'Im April 1928 wurde die Jahresversammlung von SAPU in Turku gehalten. Sven Markelius aus Stockholm war eingeladen, einen Vortrag zu halten, möglicherweise auf Aaltos und Bryggmans Bitte. Hildung Ecklund bestand darauf, dass dieser Vortrag den Durchbruch des Funktionalismus in Finnland darstelle. Im selben Sommer gingen Aino und Alvar Aalto nach Frankreich, Holland und Dänemark, um die neue Architektur zu sehen. Bryggman und Ilmari Ahonen reisten nach Deutschland, sich die Weissenhofsiedlung und Ernst Mays Wohnungsbauten in Frankfurt anzusehen und trafen in Dessau mit Gropius zusammen.

Frau Heinonen beschreibt dann Aaltos Verbindungen zu zahlreichen Wettbewerben, entweder als Teilnehmer oder als Mitglied der Jury. Sie sagt abschliessend, dass 'Alvar Aaltos Beitrag, den Funktionalismus in Finnland einzuführen, von grösster Wichtigkeit war. Er war der erste finnische Architekt, der sich mit der neuen Idelogie und Architektur vertraut machte, sie propagierte und sie in seine Gebäude assimilierte. Er scheint auch den ideologischen Gehalt des Funktionalismus erkannt zu haben, ohne auf den Fehler zu verfallen, dogmatisch seinem Programm zu folgen.'

Steven Groáks Essay behandelt drei untereinander verbundene Aspekte von Aaltos Bauten. Erstens spielt Licht bei Aalto eine dominierende Rolle – was für manche eine harmonisierende Funktion zu erfüllen scheint. Zweitens ist die Behandlung von Raumbegrenzung und das konsequente Konzept von Raum in seinen Bauten verankert, was möglich macht, eine Anzahl von Entwurfselementen zu diskutieren, das zentrale Atriummotiv, die funktionale Wegeführung, die Beschaffenheit von Aussen- und Innenwänden. Drittens gibt es seine überzeugende Handhabung von Dekoration auf allen Oberflächen, und besonders deren Rolle, diese Oberfläche in 'Schichten' erscheinen zu lassen.

Wenn man den 'Effekt der Dematerialisierung' akzeptiert, dann, so fügt Groák hinzu, '(kann) das Gebäude als Gegenstand an der Kreuzung zweier Wege gesehen werden, erstens der Weg der Sonne um das Gebäude herum und zweitens den des Betrachters, der es umschreitet und hindurchgeht. (In einem Fall nimmt das Bauwerk die Form eines Fächers an mit deutlichem Hinweis auf seinen Ursprung.) In diesem Sinn dienen alle Wände und Oberflächen gleichzeitig dazu, das Licht, das in oder auf das Gebäude fällt, zu kontrollieren, abzulenken, oder zu zerstreuen und die verschiedenen Wegeführungen zu markieren. Es ist kein Zufall, sondern eher ein besonderes Merkmal seines Entwurfs, dass viele seiner Bauten mehr als einen Eingang haben.

Wenn wir jedoch sehen, dass in vielen Fällen – aber besonders in mittleren bis grossen öffentlichen Gebäuden – ein funktionaler Wechsel in der Wegeführung durch einem Wechsel in der Ebene verdeutlicht wird, dann ist es sehr wichtig, wie und wo Treppenhäuser angelegt werden. Man könte sagen, dass Aaltos Werk eine gewisse Logik zu haben scheint, die das kleinste Detail wie auch den ganzen Bauplatz umfasst.

Um diese Idee zu testen, beschäftigt sich Groák mit Aaltos Verwendung von Dekoration. Seit den 30iger Jahren scheint Aalto in zunehmendem Masse die dekorativen Möglichkeiten von Materialien 'an sich' untersucht zu haben. Die Experimentiermauer in Muuratsalo ist wohlbekannt. Das Kraftwerk in Otaniemi erscheint fast als ein Versuch, an das Verhältnis von Wand zu Glas am Paimo Sanatorium zu erinnern.

Seine Verwendung von weissem Marmor ist interessant. Er wird in Otaniemi in erster Linie zum Markieren benutzt: er kennzeichnet den Eingang zur Bibliothek und formt jenseits des Parks eine Appliqué-Fassade an der Architekturschule, in einer Weise, die sicher als Witz gemeint ist und die auf die Vergangenheit zurückweist. Die Erforschung von Marmoroberflächen an der Finlandia Konzerthalle scheint ein grosser Erfolg zu sein. Er benutzt sie nicht nur sowohl als Abschirmung, deren Lage durch Treppen davor und dahinter bestimmt wird, als auch als reflektierende Fläche, sondern sie erlaubt ihm auch zu erkennen, dass Aalto des Gebäude konzipiert hat, zu verschiedenen Tages- und Jahreszeiten gesehen zu werden.

Er zieht den Schluss, dass in seinen Augen 'Aaltos Bauten dastehen als Gegenstände, die Systeme von Aktivitätsrouten für Menschen verbinden mit Systemen für mögliche Lichtquellen. Die Verwendung von Dekoration stellt dann Teil eines komplexen Mittels dar, durch das Wandelemente insbesondere 'dematerialisiert' sind, um diese Durchdringung und Kombinierung zu symbolisieren. Abgesehen davon erscheint Aaltos Gebrauch von Raum als 'lose' nach aussen, aber das definierend-einschliessende Gebäude ist nie wirklich transparent. Aalto bleibt seltsam, aber nicht mysteriös: es gibt genügend Bemühungen, dem Benutzer Hinweise auf die Natur seines Bauwerks zu geben.

Alvar Aalto: Sommario

Aalto rimane il più enigmatico dei maestri del Movimento Moderno. Malgrado tre grossi volumi di disegni, fotografie e dipinti di Aalto siano stati pubblicati non possiamo considerarli come l'opera completa. Egli gode fama di essere al tempo stesso un grande individualista ed uno dei due più grandi architetti Scandinavi de questo secolo, l'altro è Gunnar Asplund. E forse questa stessa fama ha impedito una discussione della totalità della sua opera, mentre gli edifici individualmente sono stati oggetto di critiche accurate e approfondite.

Dunque è giunto il momento di aprire la discussione su Aalto al livello suggerito da Venturi nel suo *Complessità e contraddizione in Architettura;* cioè affrontare i paradossi del suo lavoro che, fin dal 1927 è stato decisamente moderno, senza peraltro seguire le regole di compattezza espressiva del Movimento Moderno; cominciando col catalogare la notevole transizione di Aalto da un linguaggio vernacolare neoclassico alla sua piena espressione come Modernista. Questa stessa via fu seguita de Le Corbusier e Mies van der Rohe, della cui evoluzione parlerà un prossimo numero di *Architectural Monographs.*

Questo numero di *Architectural Monographs* è più letterario del solito poiché contiene tre significative discussioni dell'opera di Aalto. La maggior parte degli edifici è presentata dal suo studio, che continua sotto la direzione della vedova, Elissa Aalto. La produzione di questo studio fin dagli anni Venti ammonta a ben più di 300 edifici e progetti, e probabilmente se ne scopriranno altri ancora. A causa dei limiti di spazio si è fatta una selezione all'interno di questa cosí vasta opera. Il primo gruppo è formato da edifici del periodo di transizione dal vernacolo neoclassico al modernismo; in secondo luogo è l'esplorazione di un tipo, in questo caso le Biblioteche. In seguito un paragone tra la sua residenza estiva e il suo studio-ufficio, e uno dei suoi schemi per l'edilizia sociale, ed infine una scelta di edifici che mostrano il suo genio e la sua abilità; questa selezione è completata da una cronologia, la più precisa possibile.

Passiamo ora al riassunto degli articoli; Porphirios scrive: 'Propongo di schematizzare (la sensibilità ordinata che dirige il lavoro di Aalto) nelle seguenti parti, costitutive della sua produzione architettonica: 1. la sintassi planimetrica e verticale (l'organizzazione della pianta e della sezione); 2. la *taxinomia* della funzione (la classificazione del programma): la *taxinomia* della rappresentazione (l'organizzazione dei temi iconografici).'

La prima categoria della sintassi della pianta e della sezione è discussa a partire dal suo opposto dialettico: l'*omotopia,* 'il regno dell'identità', nei termini seguenti — 'Esiste una sensibilità che distribuisce la molteplicità della cose esistenti in categorie alle quali la visione ortodossa del modernismo sarebbe incapace di dare un nome, o di esprimerle o di pensarle; voglio dire il senso di ordine tutto particolare con cui i frammenti di varie combinazioni possibili si pongono separatamente senza una regola comune capace di unificarli. Questo ordine, che il razionalismo occidentale ha misconosciuto ed etichettato come disordine, noi lo chiameremo *eterotopia;* questo termine deve essere inteso nella sua accezione più letterale: cioè la condizione delle cose disposte, composte, distribuite cosí differenti tra loro che è impossibile definire un luogo comune tra tutte.'

Come esempio Porphyrios cita il 'Centro Culturale di Wolfsburg (dove) un certo numero di coesioni geometriche sembrano riunite insieme per caso: la griglia radiale delle sale di lettura, la sistemazione capovolta della biblioteca, la griglia irregolare degli uffici, le attrezzature comuni e i servizi. Qui le discontinuità sono volute; la ricerca omotopica di un ordine continuo è messa da parte e, al contrario, troviamo dei grandi sbalzi. La sintassi non ha nessuna gradualità, né sfumature. Al contrario, vuoti ed improvvise fessure precisano i limiti delle varie zone, rompendo l'edificio in frammenti sintattici, per poi riaccostarli, senza alcuna indicazione per ricostruire il rompicapo; senza lasciare dietro di sè che delle tracce difficili da decifrare.'

Utilizzando le categorie retoriche di *discriminatio* e *convenientia,* Porphyrios nota che questo modo di procedere caratterizza Richardson in America, il movimento 'Volk-Kultur-Primitiv' in Germania, la Libera Scuola Inglese e molti altri oltre agli esempi scandinavi di J. H. Palme, J. F. Willumsen e Aksel Gallen-Kallela.

La *taxinomia* della funzione in Aalto non è espressione della funzione né della struttura; 'benché a vent'anni di distanza, l'Istituto di Tecnologia di Otaniemi ha in comune col Sanatorio di Paimio la ricerca di una composizione eterotopica dei volumi. Sarebbe vano immaginare di ridurre tutto il visibile a un sistema di variabili e poi tentare di farlo corrispondere a una classificazione funzionale. Al contrario, la composizione si presenta priva di continuità essenziale; un'immagine che si pone fin dall'inizio sotto forma di frammentarietà, discontinuità, incoerenza, divergenza o discordanza;'

La *taxinomia* della rappresentazione sensuale attraverso il paragone tra Jyväskyla e la Villa Savoie a Poissy, è poi discussa in relazione al famoso cortile della residenza estiva di Aalto a Muuratsalo 'dove la grande varietà di mattoni e piastrelle si spiega liberamente come nella selvaggia profusione di una coperta *patchwork.* Questa operazione ha l'accuratezza di un dossier dove le cose sono archiviate per essere salvate dall'estinzione: qui l'immagine si spiega in tutto il suo spettacolo, mostrando le sue similitudini, le sue differenze, i suoi riferimenti o la sua materialità sensuale carica di storia.'

Porphyrios conclude che 'l'*eterotopia* . . . ha avuto un ruolo critico benché nascosto nelle scelte prioritarie della società occidentale. Al livello della sintassi della pianta e della sezione essa ha negato le codificazioni costruttive che la produzione industriale richiedeva, fungendo da difesa contro la standardizzazione assoluta dell'edilizia industrializzata e la supremazia della *techne* (tecnica nel lavoro) nella linea di montaggio. Al livello della *taxinomia* della funzione si è levata contro l'interpretazione dell'architettura come scienza invece che come arte, evitando in questo modo la sterilità quantificata del Funzionalismo così come le conseguenze sul comportamento secondario e terziario che invasero il pensiero architettonico negli anni '50 e '60, come le analisi dei dati socio-economici, le interviste degli utenti e cosí via. Al livello della *taxinomia* della rappresentazione sensibile, l'*eterotopia* si è battuta contro l'immagine imprenditoriale e l'universalità dello stile Internazionale, non per difendere il regionalismo o il nazionalismo, ma per sottolineare la non-consumabilità dell'oggetto architettonico.' Malgrado i suoi inconvenienti 'il significato della sensibilità eterotopica (di Aalto) fu, essenzialmente, che lo protese dal positivismo, nelle sue implicite alleanze contro la produzione industrializzata e lo spreco consumistico.'

L'articolo di Raija-Liisa Heinonen descrive lo sfondo dei primi anni di lavoro di Aalto: 'I paesi Scandinavi erano in stretto contatto tra di loro, non solo geograficamente ma anche linguisticamente. Il linguaggio delle persone colte in Finlandia era lo svedese . . . l'unica rivista di architettura in Finlandia *Arkkitehti-Arkitekton* era pubblicata in due edizioni, una in finlandese e l'altra in svedese . . . Tuttavia non soltanto la Svezia era divenuta importante negli Anni Venti. L'influenza dell'Italia era ancora più visibile. Il corso di studi all'Università di Tecnologia dava grande importanza al Rinascimento Italiano e al Barocco, ed è chiaro che, quando i giovani architetti viaggiavano dopo la guerra, l'Italia offriva la principale fonte d'ispirazione.' E non solo l'architettura aulica attrasse la loro attenzione, ma anche le forme cubiste del vernacolo Mediterraneo.

'Benché l'idea di far comunicare gli spazi interni con la natura derivi dall'architettura italiana, Aalto aveva anche chiaramente presenti le condizioni di vita in Finlandia, dove si passa molto tempo all'interno durante la stagione fredda. Secondo le sue stesse parole 'una casa finlandese deve avere due aspetti. Uno di essi è il contatto visivo diretto con l'esterno; l'altro, l'aspetto invernale è visibile nelle forme dell'arredamento degli interni corrispondente ai nostri sentimenti profondi'. In seguito questo motivo dell'atrio – in alcuni casi una vera piazza – appare spesso, benché con molte varianti.'

Quali furono le relazioni di questo modo di sentire con gli sviluppi internazionali? 'Nell'aprile 1928 il convegno annuale della SAFA si tenne a Turku. Sven Markelius di Stoccolma fu invitato a tenere una conferenza, probabilmente su richiesta di Aalto e Bryggman . . . Hildung Ekelund in seguito dichiarò che questa conferenza segnò l'inizio del Funzionalismo in Finlandia.' Durante l'estate 'Aino e Alvar Aalto visitarono la nuova architettura in Francia, Olanda e Danimarca. Bryggman e Ilmari Ahonen viaggiarono in Germania per visitare il quartiere di Weissenhof a Stoccarda, a Francoforte dove videro gli schemi edilizi di Ernst May e a Dessau dove incontrarono Gropius.'

R. L. Heinonen descrive poi la partecipazione di Aalto a vari concorsi come candidato o come membro della giuria. Essa conclude dicendo che 'il contributo di Alvar Aalto all'introduzione del Funzionalismo in Finlandia fu della più grande importanza. Egli fu il primo architetto finlandese a trovarsi d'accordo con la nuova ideologia architettonica, a diffonderla ed assimilarla nei suoi edifici. Egli sembra anche aver realizzato i contenuti ideologici del funzionalismo, senza peraltro perdersi in una ricopiatura dogmatica del suo programma.'

L'articolo di Steven Groák descrive tre aspetti collegat degli edifici di Aalto. In primo luogo il ruolo dominante della luce nel lavoro di Aalto, vista da alcuni in una funzione armonizzante. In secondo luogo il modo di trattare l'involucro e la conseguente concezione dello spazio incorporato negli edifici, il che permette la discussione di vari elementi di progettoil motivo dell'atrio centrale, la 'strada' funcionale, e la natura dei percorsi interni ed esterni. E infine c'è l'uso frequente della decorazione su tutte le superfici e, in particolare, il suo ruolo nel creare una 'stratificazione' di queste superfici.'

Se l'effetto dematerializzante è ben noto, Groák aggiunge poi che 'gli edifici (possono) essere visti come oggetti all'intersezione di due percorsi- quello del sole attorno all'edificio e quello dell'osservatore che segue un cammino attorno e attraverso l'edificio (e talvolta la forma costruita è ugualmente generata come un 'ventaglio', con un significato conseguente all'origine). In questo senso, tutti i muri e le superfici servono simultaneamente a controllare, deviare o ridistribuire la luce che cade all'interno o sull'edificio e a segnare i vari percorsi. Non è una coincidenza ma anzi una particolarità corrispondente a questo proposito, che molti degli edifici abbiano varie entrate. Tuttavia, se osserviamo che in molte occasioni -ma specialmente negli edifici pubblici medi e grandi- un cambiamento di funzione del percorso è segnato da un cambiamento di livello, allora diventa molto importante come e dove sono disposte le scale.' Possiamo cosí vedere che l'opera di Aalto può interpretarsi come guidata da una logica che governa il più piccolo particolare cosí come il piano generale.

Per verificare questa idea Groák prende in considerazione l'uso della decorazione in Aalto.' Dal 1930 in poi, Aalto sembra aver cercato sempre più le possibilità decorative dei materiali 'in se stessi'. Il muro sperimentale di Muuratsalo è ben noto. La Centrale Elettrica di Otaniemi va letta quasi come un tentativo di evocare la scala del volume solido in contrasto con il vetro del Sanatorio di Paimio. Anche il suo uso del marmo bianco è molto interessante. E' usato a Otaniemi principalmente come un riferimento -esso identifica l'entrata della biblioteca e, attraverso il parco, forma una facciata applicata sulla Scuola di Architettura in un modo che è certamente una deliberata ironia, in riferimento al passato. L'esplorazione delle superfici marmoree nella Sala da Concerti Finlandia sembra un successo totale. Non soltanto il marmo è usato al tempo stesso come schermo, presso le scale sul lato e sulla facciata, e come una superficie riflettente, ma anche permette di comprendere che Aalto concepiva l'edificio come visto in molti diversi momenti del giorno e dell'anno.'

Egli conclude che ai suoi occhi 'gli edifici di Aalto . . . esistono come oggetti che combinano sistemi di percorsi funzionali e il sistema delle possibili sorgenti luminose. L'uso della decorazione fa parte di questo complesso di significati per cui gli elementi murari in particolare sono 'dematerializzati' appunto per simboleggiare questa penetrazione e combinazione. L'uso dello spazio in Aalto appare 'fluido' ai bordi, ma l'edificio definitochiuso, non è mai veramente trasparente. Esso rimane insolito ma forse non misterioso: è molto importante dare all'utente spiegazioni sulla natura dell'edificio.'

Alvar Aalto: Resumen

Aalto ha permanecido uno de los grandes más enigmáticos del Movimiento Moderno. Tres grandes volúmenes se han publicado con sus dibujos, fotografías y pinturas, pero todavía estan lejos de ser la obra completa. Aalto tiene una aura de ser un gran individualista y a la misma vez uno de los dos arquitectos escandinavos más importantes, el otro arquitecto siendo Gunnar Asplund. Quizas ésta aura ha obscurecido una discusión de toda su obra, aún cuando ciertos edificios individuales han recibido crítica cuidadosa y penetrante.

Ahora es cuando se discute a Aalto como lo sugiere Venturi en su libro *Complexity and Contradiction in Architecture*; eso es, ceder a las paradojas de su obra que desde 1927 son definitivamente modernas sin obedecer las reglas de consistencia y expresión que eran corrientes del Movimiento Moderno; se ha empezado a catalogar la increible transición de Aalto como arquitecto neo-clásico vernacular a su florecimiento como Modernista. Este camino tambien fué tomado por Le Corbusier y Mies van der Rohe, una transición que una futura edición de *Architectural Monographs* intenta estudiar.

Esta edición de *Architectural Monographs* es más literaria que de costumbre y contiene tres importantes discusiones sobre los aspectos de la obra de Aalto. Aún más edificios se construiran, ya que su oficina continua bajo la dirección de su viuda, la Sra Elissa Aalto. La producción de tal oficina desde los años veinte cuenta con unos 300 edificios y proyectos, y todavía hay posibilidades de descubrirs más. Por limitaciones de espacio, sólo se ha incluido una pequena selección de ésta obra extensa. La primera agrupación de edificios consiste en aquellos del periodo de transición del neo-clásico vernacular al Modernismo; la segunda estudia la exploración de un tipo de edificio, en este caso las bibliotecas. Luego su casa de verano y su oficina/estudio se compara con un esquema de vivienda agregada, y finalmente seleccionamos una serie de edificios que demuestran su genio y habilidad; esta sección termina con una cronología tan completa como es corrientemente posible.

Resumiendo los articulos, Demetri Porphyrios escribe: 'Propongo delinear (la sensibilidad de orden que se encuentra en toda la obra de Aalto) las zonas ensenciales de producción arquitectónica: particularmente 1. la sintaxis planimétrica y seccional (la organización del plan y la sección); 2. la *taxinomia* de función (la clasificación del programa); la *taxinomia* de la representación sensual (la organización de los temas iconográficos)'.

La primera categoría de la sintaxis planimétrica y seccional se discute despues de plantear el dialecto opuesto de *homotopia* 'el reino de lo igual' en los términos siguientes — 'Existe una sensibilidad que distribuye la multiplicidad de lo existente en categorías que la mirada ortodoxa del Modernismo es incapaz de nombrar, hablar ni pensar; quiero decir ese sentido de orden en el cual fragmentos de un número posible de coherencias brillan separadamente sin una ley común que las unan. Ese orden, que el racionalismo occidental ha desconfiado y lo ha llamado desorden, lo llamaremos *heterotopia*; ésta palabra se ha de tomar literalmente: es decir, el estado de lo colocado, lo puesto, lo asignado en sitios tan diferentes uno del otro que es imposible definir un lugar común subrayándoles.'

Como ejemplo, Porphyrios cita el 'Cento Cultural Wolfsburg [en donde] un cierto número de coherencias geométricas parecen haberse unido al azar: la red radial de las salas de conferencias, el arreglo introvertido de la biblioteca, y la red ortogonal desigual de las oficinas, las utilidades públicas y lugares auxiliares. En éste caso las descontinuaciones se acogen. El requisito homotópico de un orden continuo se ha rechazado y en su lugar se han introducido grandes saltos. La sintaxis no está graduada, nunca sombreada. En su lugar, espacios vacios y aberturas imprevistas circunscriben los límites de cada zona, dividiendo el edificio en fragmentos sintácticos, y luego yuxtaponiéndo las fragmentos; sin dar pistas que quizás expliquen el rompecabezas perdido; no dejando nada más que huellas difíciles de descifrar.'

Utilizando las categorías retóricas de *discriminatio* y *convenientia*, Porphyrios nota que éste camino caracteriza a Richardson en América, el *Volk-Kultur-Primitiv* en Alemania, el *Free School* inglés y muchos otros, pero escoge los ejemplos escandinavos de J. H. Palme, J. F. Willumsen y Aksel Gallen-Kallela.

La *taxinomia* de función con Aalto es no es expresión de función ni de estructura; 'al mismo tiempo, aún despues de veintiocho años aparte, el Instituto de Tecnología de Otaniemi comparte, con el Sanatorio de Paimio el mismo deseo de una composición volumétrica heterotópica. Sería inútil reducir toda un aspecto de lo visible a un sistema de variables y luego intentar conectarlas con una clasificación funcional. En cambio, la composición se presenta sin continuación esencial; la visibilidad se afirma desde el comienzo en forma de fragmentación, discontinuidad, contradicción, divergencia o desordenación.'

La *taxinomia* de la representación sensual se discute comparando a Jyväskyla y la Villa Savoie en Poissy con el famoso patio de la casa de verano de Aalto en Muuratsalo 'donde la gran veriedad de filas alternantes de ladrillo y baldosas se exhibe abiertamente a la manera de un *patchwork quilt*. Esto es lo sobresaliente de la conciencia del *dossier* en donde las cosas se guardan para ser salvadas de extinción; es aquí donde lo visible se despliega espectacularmente, mostrando las similaridades, las diferencias, las leyendas relacionadas, o su materialidad cargada de historia sensual.'

Porphyrios concluye que '*heterotopia* . . . jugó una parte silenciosa confrontada con las prioridades de la sociedad occidental. Al nivel de la sintáxis planimétrica y seccional la heterotopía negaba los códigos de construcción que la producción industrial necesitaba, resguardándolo contra una completa reducción a un tipo establecido de industria de construccion y el traspaso al *techne* (la técnica en trabajo) de serie. Al nivel de la *taxinomia* de función, se mantuvo contra la interpretación de arquitectura como ciencia en vez de arte, así eludiendo la esterilidad del Funcionalismo y sus consecuencias secundarias y terciarias que a tormentaron el pensamiento arquitectónico de los años cincuenta y sesenta, y el análisis de data socioeconómica, las entrevistas con el consumidor y lo demás. Al nivel de la *taxinomia* de la representación sensual, *heterotopia* luchó contra la imágen empresaria y la universalidad del estilo Internacional, no para defender regionalismo ni nacionalismo, sino que para subrayar lo no consumible del objeto arquitectónico'. A pesar de sus desventajas 'la importancia de la sensibilidad heterotópica (de Aalto) era, basicamente, esa de positivismo protegido, con las alianzas implícitas de ésta hacia la producción industrializada y los desperdicios del consumidor'.

El artículo de Raija-Liisa Heinonen describe los primeros años ejerciendo su práctica; 'Los paises escandinavos estan cercanamente relacionados, no sólo geográficamente pero tambien ligüisticamente. La lengua cultural en Finlandia era sueco . . . la única revista arquitectónica en Finlandia *Arkkitehti-Arkitekton* se publicaba en dos ediciones distintas, uno en finlandés y el otro en sueco . . . Pero no sólo Suecia se volvió importante en los años veinte. La influencia de Italia era mucho más obvia. El plan de estudios en la Universidad de Tecnología daba énfasis al renacimiento italiano y al barroco, y claramente quando los jóvenes arquitectos viajaron despues de la guerra, Italia era *la* fuente de inspiración.' No sólo les atraían los grandes edificios pero tambien las formas vernanculares cúbicas del Mediterráneo.

'Aún cuando la idea de unir el interior con la naturaleza deriva de la arquitectura italiana, Aalto consideró las condiciones finlandesas en donde se pasa mucho tiempo en el interior durante los meses de invierno. Según él 'la casa finlandesa debe tener dos caras. Una de ellas tiene contacto directo estético con el exterior; otro, la cara de invierno, se ve mediante el diseño interior que corresponde con los sentimientos más profundos'. Más tarde el tema del atrio aparece a menudo pero con muchas variaciones.

¿Y éste sentimiento cómo se relaciona con los desarrollos internacionales? 'En abril de 1928 la reunión anual de la SAFA se celebró en Turku. Sven Markelius de Estocolmo fue invitado a dar una conferencia probablemente a petición de Aalto y Bryggman . . . más tarde Hildung Ekelund declaró que ésta conferencia señaló la introducción del Funcionalismo en Finlandia'. Durante ese verano 'Aino y Alvar Aalto fueron a Francia, Holanda y Dinamarca para ver la nueva arquitectura. Bryggman y Ilmari Ahonen fueron a Alemania visitando el Weissenhofseidlung en Stuttgart, Frankfurt donde vieron el proyecto de viviendas de Ernst May y Dessau donde conocieron a Gropius'.

La Sra Heinonen después describe las conexiones de Aalto como participante o juez en competiciones. Concluye que 'la contribución de Aalto en introducir el Funcionalismo en Finlandia fué muy importante. Fué el primer arquitecto finlandés en conocer la nueva ideología y arquitectura, en difundirlo y asimilarlo en sus edificios. También se dió cuenta de el contenido del Funcionalismo sin errar dogmaticamente siguiendo el programa.'

El artículo de Steven Gróak se interesa en tres aspectos relacionados de los edificios de Aalto. 'Primero hay el papel dominante de la luz – que para unos cuantos desempeña una función armonizante. Segundo está el tratamiento de lo encerrado y la concepción del espacio incorporado en los edificios, que permite el discurso de varios elementos de planificación – el atrio central la ruta funcional, y el carácter de las paredes internas y externas. Tercero está el uso persuasivo de la decoración de todas las superficies y en particular su papel en crear un 'estrato' de esas superficies.

Si la definición de 'efecto dematerializador' se acepta, entonces Gróak añade que 'los edificios pueden considerarse como objetos en el cruce de dos rutas, una del sol alrededor del edificio y la otra del observador alrededor del edificio. (Y a veces la forma construida parcialmente engendra una forma de abanico.) En éste sentido, todas las paredes y superficies simultáneamente controlan, desconciertan o redistribuyen la luz que entra o está sobre el edificio marcando las varias rutas. No es coincidencia sino que un atributo de ésta proposición de que hayan varias entradas. En varios casos, sobre todo en los edificios públicos de tamaño mediano y grande, la ruta funcional se distingue con un cambio de nivel haciendo importante la colocación de las escaleras'. Así podemos ver que la obra de Aalto puede ser interpretada como tener una lógica que cubre hasta los detalles más pequeños hasta aquellos del plan de situación.

Examinando ésta idea, Gróak considera el uso de la decoración de Aalto. 'Apartir de 1930, Aalto investigó las posibilidades decorativas de los materiales 'mismos'. La pared experimental en Muuratsalo es conocida. La estación generadora de Otaniemi puede a veces leerse como una tentativa de evocar una escala solida *versus* el vidrio del Sanatorio de Paimio. Su uso de mármol blanco es interesante. En Otaniemi lo usa como señal, identifica la entrada a la biblioteca y al otro lado del parque crea una fachada de la Escuela de Arquitectura. La exploración de las superficies de mármol en la Sala de Conciertos Finlandia estan muy bien logradas. No sólo se utiliza como mampara, al lado de las escaleras y en frente de ellas, y como superficie reflejante, pero también demuestra que Aalto concebió elde ver el edificio durante las diferencias estaciones del día y del año.

Concluye que para él 'los edificios de Aalto . . . existen como objetos que combinan sistemas de rutas de actividades para personas y un posible sistema de fuente de luz. Siendo así, el uso de decoración es una parte de un método complejo en el cual las paredes se dematerializan para simbolizar esta penetración y combinación. Mas allá de éste enfoque . . . el uso de espacio parece 'suelto' en los bordes, pero el edificio definido/encerrado nunca es transparente. Se mantiene estraño pero no misterioso: hay un interés en dar al usador pistas para entender el carácter de sus edificios.